£1

The First Christ~~mas~~

Hubert John Richards was born in 1921. He studied for the Roman Catholic priesthood at the English College in Rome, where he took his degree in Theology in 1946 and in Scripture in 1948. From 1949 to 1965 he taught Sacred Scripture to students for the priesthood at St Edmund's College, Ware. In 1965 he was appointed principal of the newly founded Corpus Christi College in London, an international institute of religious education. He retired from this post in 1972.

He is widely known, both in England and abroad, as a lecturer on the problems of religious education, and as a composer of a variety of gospel songs. He is the author of: *God Speaks to Us, Christ in Our World* (with Peter De Rosa), *What the Spirit Says to the Churches, An ABC of the Bible, Forty Gospel Songs, Ten Gospel Songs, The Heart of a Rose.*

D0582966

THE
FIRST CHRISTMAS
What Really Happened?

Hubert J. Richards

COLLINS
Fontana Books

First published in Fontana Books 1973
© Hubert J. Richards 1973

Printed in Great Britain
Collins Clear-Type Press
London and Glasgow

Acknowledgements

The author and publisher wish to thank the
Hutchinson Publishing Group Ltd. for their kind
permission to use copyright material from *Borstal
Boy* by Brendan Behan.

Scriptural quotations are taken from *The
Jerusalem Bible* (copyright © 1966 by Darton,
Longman & Todd, Ltd. and Doubleday and
Company, Inc. Used by permission of the publisher), but the author has felt free occasionally
to depart from this when the nuance of the argument required it.

Contents

1. Foreword

I recently came across a translation of a passage from the Old Testament book of Ecclesiastes. It ran as follows:

> Objective consideration of contemporary phenomena compels the conclusion that success or failure in competitive activities exhibits no tendency to be commensurate with innate capacity, but that a considerable element of the unpredictable must invariably be taken into account.

Anyone who knows that the original reads quite simply:

> I see this too under the sun . . . all things are subject to time and chance (Ecclesiastes 9:11)

will appreciate the wry point George Orwell was making in this playful exercise in translation in his *Essay on Politics and the English Language*. The best way to hide the meaning of what anyone is saying is to wrap it up in verbose and technical language.

Most books of theology are written in technical language. Some are verbose as well. Many of them, translated from a foreign tongue in order to make them available to English readers, need to be mentally translated back into their original before they will yield their meaning. The net result is that what theologians are saying rarely reaches the general public.

With some theologians this is perhaps no great loss. But that this should be the general situation is deplorable. It is as if people were still trying to work out complicated mathematical problems on an abacus after computers had been invented. Or attempting to steer ships round the world on the supposition that the earth is flat.

The extent of the gulf that separates the ordinary Christian from the agreed conclusions of theologians can be gauged from the fact that so many Christians still feel it rather disloyal to suggest that the world was not literally created in six days. If that is what the Bible says, how can anyone who questions it call himself a Christian? Yet that particular battle was fought and concluded a hundred years ago, and even official Church documents have incorporated the theologians' judgement that the first chapter of Genesis not only may but *must* be interpreted as a piece of poetry. Not that poetry does not embody a truth, but it is a truth of a different kind from that conveyed by a literal description of events.

How does it come to be that this kind of news takes so long to filter through to the ordinary man in the pew? Who is to blame for the blockage? Is it the obscure language of the theologians themselves? Is it the excessively guarded language of the official documents, which are so reluctant to admit the limitedness and inadequacy of past statements that it is only those who have read the past statements who realize how different some later statements can be? Is it the failure of the communicators (preachers, teachers, lecturers) to convey these conclusions to their charges, or even to be aware of them themselves? Is it the general resistance to change which affects everyone in matters of religion? Whichever it is, the long term result is that many people live their Christianity at a primitive and naïve level of thinking which they would not tolerate in any other area of their lives.

Of course, for those whose religion is a world apart, a kind of ghetto into which they escape from the harsh reality of everyday living, no great harm can ensue; the gulf merely illustrates the reality of their situation. But those who are concerned to maintain some continuity between their religion and their everyday lives in a twentieth-century world may find that such straddling is beyond their acrobatic ability. And if every attempt to bridge the gulf for them is suspected or censured or sabotaged, who shall blame them if they lose their faith?

It has always been my desire to build bridges, not only between faith and life (indeed that work has often already been done very well by others), but especially between the theologians who have done that work and those who are unaware of it. I realize that this makes my task one of popularization rather than of creative theology. I claim no real originality for any part of this book. But then neither the original theologian nor the popularizer can afford to neglect each other; indeed if the result of the theologian's work is not made public he is wasting his time.

I realize too that the popularizer is in danger of oversimplifying issues which are always more complex than his brief allows him to reveal, else he would be defeating his own purpose. But, being aware of the danger, I can only hope that I have avoided it, and leave it to theologians to judge whether I have succeeded.

I realize finally that anyone who has, whether by design or by chance, been kept well insulated from the work of theologians over the last hundred years, may suffer some initial shock when he is first exposed to their findings. I can only offer as consolation my own experience of several generations of students, that the initial shock, far from weakening their faith, has invariably strengthened it, rather as the shock experienced by a babe newly expelled from its protective womb, where it longs to stay but where it would die, enables it to live.

This book deals only with the gospel stories on the

birth and childhood of Jesus. Much theological work has been done in this area since the beginning of this century, mostly by non-Catholics. Catholic theologians did not enter the field until the 1950's, and a cynic might be forgiven for asking whether this was simply another example of Catholics, some reluctantly, some gratefully, jumping on to a bandwagon whose progress they could no longer prevent. But in actual fact, although at that time they largely accepted the conclusions about the nature of these stories which their non-Catholic colleagues had arrived at long before, the Catholic scholars had their own contribution to make, especially on the scriptural background of the stories, and the light which can be thrown on their purpose and meaning by a study of parallel stories from the Old Testament.

It is this purpose and meaning of the infancy stories which I am concerned to explain in this book. Because apart from the minor palpitations which any popular presentation of the subject seems to be capable of arousing, most people calmly continue to read the gospel infancy stories with a naïve literalism, as if no scholarly work had ever been done on them. The aim of the chapters which follow is simply to make that scholarly work available to a wide public, so that they should be aware that there is not only one approach to the gospel stories, nor only one way of understanding them. It goes without saying, therefore, that I would not wish to impose any of the views expressed in this book. Such a 'new orthodoxy' would be as objectionable as the old, which has often successfully prevented many people from ever coming to meet the Christ for whom they were searching.

2. The Christmas Stories
Fact or Fiction?

The term 'Christmas stories' is used here to refer to the opening pages of the gospels of St Matthew and St Luke, which both recount a number of stories about the birth and childhood of Jesus. This chapter simply wants to ask some general questions about these stories.

ADDITIONS TO THE GOSPEL

I presume that the first question one should ask about the Christmas stories is, 'How did they come to form part of the gospel story?'

Many people will feel that the question should be put the other way round : not, 'How did Matthew and Luke come to add these stories?' but, 'How did Mark and John come to leave them out?' But the fact is that the original gospel, that is to say, the *preached* 'good news' of which the written gospels are only expanded versions, always begins the story of Jesus' life with his baptism by John. This we can check from the Acts of the Apostles, which reconstructs a number of the earliest Christian sermons, and all of them presume that the coming of Jesus was heralded not by angels but by John the Baptist, and that to tell of his life one should begin not at Bethlehem but at Jordan. (See Peter's summary of the life of Jesus : 'from the time when John was baptizing until the day when he was taken up from us', Acts 1 :22; Peter's address to the household of Cornelius : '... about

Jesus of Nazareth and how he began in Galilee, after John had been preaching baptism', Acts 10 :37; Paul's preaching to the Jews of Antioch : 'God has raised up . . . Jesus, as Saviour, whose coming was heralded by John when he proclaimed a baptism of repentance', Acts 13 :23-4). Indeed this is the supposition lying behind the composition of both our earliest and our latest gospel : the opening stories in both Mark and John tell of Jesus' baptism, and no attempt is made to describe anything that is presumed to have happened before.

The Christmas stories, then, far from being the earliest part of the gospel, as their position at the beginning would suggest, seem to be the latest. The earliest preaching about Jesus concentrated on his public life. How did these stories about his 'hidden life' come to be added?

PIOUS FICTION?

It would be tempting to answer this question by comparing the stories with the many pseudonymous or 'apocryphal' writings which, towards the end of the first century and the beginning of the second, began to grow wild, as it were, out of the crevices in the biblical writings. (A selection of infancy stories from the apocryphal writings will be found below, in chapter 5.) There are any number of passages in both the Old Testament and the New which leave the kind of gap which an inventive writer could feel called upon to fill in with a piece of pious fiction. For instance, an apocryphal but very beautiful *Prayer of Manasseh* has 'grown' out of the gap left in the curt reference to the conversion of a wicked Israelite king in 2 Chronicles 33 :13. Or again, the detailed description of Mary's virginity, purporting to be based on eye-witness reports and first-hand evidence, in the *Protogospel of James* has evidently been prompted by the lack of detail on the subject offered by Luke 1:34, which says no more than 'I am a virgin.' The dozens of stories of Jesus' boyhood contained in the *Gospel of Thomas* (including the famous ones of the sparrows made of mud which come to life and fly when Jesus claps his hands, and the piece of wood cut too short by Joseph and stretched to the right size by Jesus) are presumably an attempt to fill in the gap left by the canonical gospels, which offer us only one story about the boy Jesus – his pilgrimage to Jerusalem – in Luke 2:41-50. A whole series of *Acts* recounting the journeys and exploits of a number of the apostles (the *Quo Vadis* story of Peter running away from persecution in Rome, and his meeting with a Christ who offers to take his place to be crucified again, come from such writings) must have arisen out of the fact that the New Testament Acts of the Apostles, in spite of its title, offers information in the long run about Paul alone.

Are the Christmas stories the same kind of literature – pious fiction based on the fact that no real information existed, written merely to edify or entertain?

THEOLOGY

That would certainly be to underrate them. Close examination has revealed that they are made of far more serious stuff, that they in fact embody a whole theology.

For the Christmas stories are not the only ones in the gospel which deal with the 'hidden' life of Jesus, that is to say, with episodes for which there were no witnesses. The agony in the garden, for instance, is said to have taken place while the only available witnesses, Peter, James and John, were asleep. How then describe such a scene? A study of the texts shows that they have simply expanded the words of the 'Our Father'. This is how Jesus had taught his disciples to pray; how else would he, in this moment of agonizing decision, address himself to God except in terms of 'Father . . . thy will be done . . . an angel from heaven . . . pray that you may not enter into temptation'? (Luke 22 :42-6)

Similarly the temptation with which the first three gospels open their account of Jesus' public life is something in which, by the nature of things, Jesus alone was involved. How then write about such a hidden aspect of Jesus' life? The fourth gospel has preserved a record of the actual circumstances in Jesus' public life which seem to lie behind the story. It tells of the feeding of the multitude in the desert, their attempt to acclaim him as king, and the subsequent suggestion of his disciples that he manifest himself not only in Galilee but in Jerusalem as well (John 6 : 1-15, 7 : 1-8). That is how Jesus' struggle with Satan took place at the historical level. In a more stylized manner, Matthew, Mark and Luke have used this material for the opening page of their gospels, to speak of a Jesus tempted to produce bread miraculously in the desert, to seize the power of kingship, and to manifest himself in the Jerusalem temple.

In other words, the stories are theological rather than factual or biographical. This does not mean that they are less valuable or less true. On the contrary, they convey something deeply true about Jesus, because they are a reflection on the meaning of the whole of his life, not simply of one episode. And the Christmas stories belong to this same category.

KINGDOM COME

If one wanted to press the point further and specify what sort of theology the Christmas stories represent, one would have to use the difficult term 'eschatological theology'.

The word *eschata* refers to the last things, or 'kingdom come'. There is plenty of evidence in the New Testament that the first generation of Christians, bewildered by the fact that Jesus' life and ministry did not seem to live up to the Old Testament promises of 'kingdom come', looked forward to a *second* coming when Christ would return in glory to execute God's last judgement.

It is the concern of the later writings of the New Testament, like St John's gospel, the last epistles of St Paul, and the Christmas stories here under discussion, to suggest that these expectations, if they were expressed in any exclusive sense, were misdirected. For the kingdom really had come in the death and resurrection of Jesus which, rightly seen, was already the promised return of Christ and the day of judgement. In fact, the kingdom had come even before that, in the public life inaugurated at Jesus' baptism which, rightly seen, was already the coming of Christ in glory, a sort of enactment of his death and resurrection in miniature. Indeed, the kingdom had come even earlier than that, in the *first* coming of Jesus at his birth which, rightly seen, should have revealed to the eyes of faith all that his subsequent life and death was to make plain.

If it is this kind of theological thinking which is embodied in the Christmas stories, how strange to treat them as if they were simply sweet little stories for the children. The infancy stories of Jesus are first of all for adults.

WHAT IS A MIDRASH?

Because this theological thinking is done on the basis of a number of Old Testament texts, as we shall see in more detail below, these opening chapters of Matthew and Luke are nowadays often spoken of as *midrash*. It is not a euphonious word, but it is in fact the technical term for a certain type of interpretation of scripture.

The word *darash* means to examine, or study, or meditate. *Midrash* is that kind of examination and meditation of the Old Testament which grew up among the Jews in the sixth century B.C. when, exiled in Babylonia and stripped of everything that had previously distinguished them from the peoples among whom they lived, their sacred books took on a new significance. In the conviction that God's word once spoken was valid for all time and not only for its first recipients, and in the certainty that God was consistent and would not do anything in the future which contradicted what he had done in the past, they did not hesitate to search the ancient scriptures for an understanding of their own very different circumstances.

This, after all, was what God had said; therefore it applied to them too. This, after all, was what God had done, and therefore it must contain an outline of what he would do for them. The past must throw light on the present.

In this way, a whole new tradition not only of re-reading but of *retelling* the Bible grew up, in which the old texts were deliberately rewritten to make them applicable and relevant to new circumstances. Stories which once had reference only to past events were annotated and elaborated so that they would refer more explicitly to the present. The school in which this study was done began to be known, as Jewish schools still are, as *Beth Hammidrash*, the House for Searching the Scriptures.

The literary form of *midrash* is a strange one. Old materials are being used to construct a deliberately new building. The topic under discussion is always basically a present event, but it is being described in terms borrowed entirely from the past. To read a *midrash* is to be exposed constantly to a double image, where the past is often indistinguishable from the present, and where the event being depicted can no longer be distinguished from the colours which have been used to paint it.

Some of the literature recently found among the Dead Sea Scrolls is of this kind, a rewriting and embellishment of Old Testament texts to make them more relevant to the second century B.C. in which the Qumran sect lived. Many of the later books in the Old Testament, when 'inspiration' and originality were at a low ebb, are simply a reformulation and reworking of material from older books. The final chapters of the book of Wisdom offer one of the clearest examples, where the text of the book of Exodus is taken up and embellished in the most overt manner to make it more directly applicable to the circumstances of its Jewish readers in the Egypt of 50 B.C., in passages like the following:

The godless who refused to acknowledge you
were scourged by the strength of your arm,
pursued by no ordinary rains, hail and unrelenting
    downpours,
and consumed by fire.
Even more wonderful, in the water – which quenches
    all –
the fire raged fiercer than ever;

for the elements fight for the virtuous.

At one moment the flame would die down,

to avoid consuming the animals sent against the godless

and to make clear to them by that sight, that the
sentence of God was pursuing them;

at another, in the very heart of the water, it would
burn more fiercely than fire

to ruin the harvests of a guilty land.

How differently with your people! You gave them the
food of angels,

from heaven untiringly sending them bread already
prepared,

containing every delight, satisfying every taste.

And the substance you gave demonstrated your sweet-
ness towards your children,

for, conforming to the taste of whoever ate it,

it transformed itself into what each eater wished.

                                        (Wisdom 16 : 16-21)

Since the Christmas stories are based on the Old Testament in something of the same way, using the past to
throw light on the present, and leaving the reader un-
certain how to distinguish the historical facts from the
background against which they are presented, they are
very often referred to today by the same term, *midrash*.

A BETTER DESCRIPTION

It is obviously a legitimate use of the word *midrash*.
However, since the word is used to cover a very wide
variety of narratives, including some that are quite
trivial, it is perhaps not the best word to apply to the
opening chapters of Matthew and Luke, which can be

more accurately described as Christian meditations on the Old Testament.

A truly Christian reading of the Old Testament will approach it not simply as a long preparation *for* Christ, but as a constant anticipation *of* Christ. The Christian should be able to see that the Old Testament and the New are not two disparate realities, as if God first tried a whole number of different shifts, and finally in exasperation abandoned them in order to give us Christ. Christ is of the same nature as the various realities of the Old Testament. They were all, like him, the word of God which finally, in him, took flesh and blood.

It is therefore legitimate for the Christian to see Christ *in* the Old Testament descriptions of temple and prophetism and priesthood and kingship and the rest. In fact it is essential that he should do so. If he cannot, he can gain nothing from reading the Old Testament : the New Testament would have made it irrelevant. The Christian is not committed to a faith different from that of a Jew. The Christian who cannot see that his faith is the same as the Jew's is being untrue to Jesus. He was in no doubt about the Jewish faith he professed !

It would seem best, therefore, in trying to describe what sort of literature the Christmas stories are, to speak of them quite simply as meditations on Old Testament themes, done by people who saw the risen Christ as the fullest expression of those themes.

THEOLOGICAL QUESTIONS

What conclusions, then, ought one to draw at this stage of our discussion? First of all that we should treat the opening chapters of Matthew and Luke respectfully for what they are, stories which embody a theology. This means that the only legitimate questions we may ask of these chapters are theological ones.

In this respect it might be helpful to draw a parallel with the opening chapters of the book of Genesis. There was a time when we came to these chapters of the Bible expecting answers to such historical and scientific questions as, '*When* was the world created? *How* did it come into being? *What* is the world made of? *Where* did man first appear?' We no longer ask these questions of Genesis because we have come to see that the writer is a theologian, not a scientist, and that he never intended to pose or answer questions of this kind. He is concerned with the much more profound questions, '*What kind* of world do we live in? *What kind* of persons should we be?'

In something of the same way we ought to realize that in their opening pages Matthew and Luke do not offer us information but theology. They are concerned to tell us not *how* and *where* and *when* Jesus was born and grew up, but *who* Jesus is. And to this question they always give the same answer : he is the crucified one who was raised from the dead and lives on to give life to all who believe in him.

We do not perhaps sufficiently appreciate how basic to the whole presentation of Jesus in the gospel is the fact of his resurrection. We sometimes treat the resurrection as if it was an unexpected bonus added on to the end of the gospel story, whereas it is, of course, ultimately the only message that the evangelist has to preach. This means that the risen Christ is to the forefront of the evangelist's mind throughout, necessarily influencing the way in which he is going to speak of Jesus. In the light of the sequel towards which the whole story is directed, and which is indeed the whole point of the story, all the facts of Jesus' earthly life are seen in retrospect to have an extra dimension, and this cannot be expressed in the kind of terms recorded by a camera or a cassette, only in symbolism and imagery. We should expect such symbolic language in this sort of writing, not be surprised at it. It is the only language in which profound theological realities can be expressed.

That this goes for the opening pages of the gospel as much as for any other page, is well put by C. H. Dodd in his recent masterly study of the New Testament, *The Founder of Christianity* (Collins, London, 1971, pp. 30-1; Fontana, p. 42):

Symbols and images . . . cluster thickly in the scenes of the 'Christmas story' which in Matthew and Luke is the prelude to their account of the public career of Jesus : visits of angels, prophetic dreams, the marvellous star in the east, the miraculous birth greeted with songs from the heavenly choir, all the appealing incidents so familiar in the appropriate setting of Christmas carol and nativity play. That there is a basis of fact somewhere behind it all need not be doubted, but he would be a bold man who should presume to draw a firm line between fact and symbol. What our authors are saying through all this structure of imagery is that the obscure birth of a child to a carpenter's wife was, in view of all that came out of it, a decisive moment in history, when something genuinely new began, and the traffic of two worlds was initiated, to be traced by the discerning eye all through the story that was to follow.

BIOGRAPHICAL QUESTIONS

If the Christmas stories, then, are theology rather than plain description, and if only theological questions are in order, it follows that biographical questions are out of place. That this is not sufficiently understood is obvious from the sort of questions which any treatment of these stories persistently arouses, from the sophisticated as well as the simple: 'Why did Joseph . . .? When did Mary . . .? How did Jesus . . .? Whom did Herod . . .? Where did the Magi . . .?' Yet if these chapters are a theological reflection on the meaning of Christ's life, to ask such questions is not only to misunderstand them, but to belittle, to discredit, and ultimately to ruin them.

A child – and a childlike age – will be content to explore the meaning of a story without inquiring closely about its historical character. An adult – and the history-conscious age in which we live – will want to distinguish very clearly between the historical and the non-historical. Not in order to keep one and reject the other, but to appreciate the kind of truth with which the story is concerned. And if the writer of a story never intended it to be read as a piece of scientific history, then to defend its historicity against all comers is to invite many people to reject it. To give the poetic elements of the story a biographical character is to make the story so unreal for many people that they will want nothing more to do with it. Far from rescuing the story, we would have destroyed it. John Robinson puts the point in these words in *But That I Can't Believe* (Fontana, London, 1967, p. 28):

Many today are put off by a way of thinking which was no stumbling-block at all to the men of the Bible. They naturally thought of God as 'up there' or 'out there', and the idea of a heavenly Being 'sending' his Son to this world was perfectly acceptable to an age which thought of gods paying visits to the earth. This is where you looked for reality to be revealed. But to most people to-day that just seems fanciful, and makes the whole Christmas story sound like a fairy-tale. I am much more concerned that it shall ·sound like the reality it is than that we should preserve the time-honoured pictures. If it helps to say that in Jesus reality comes through, rather than comes down, then by all means let's say it.

Then there are all the 'tinselly' bits of the Christmas story – the star, the angels and the celestial choir. These were recognized ways for the men of the Bible of saying 'God is in all this'. As poetry, I believe, they still have a magic power to take us out of our mean selves. They speak of the mystery of Christmas. But if all they succeed in doing for you is banishing Christ to an unreal world of fairy-lights, then cut them out.

The kind of biographical questions which we keep putting to the scriptures, New Testament as well as Old, are in fact secondary, not primary. The first thing that should be in our mind when we read any page of the gospel is that this is a profession of faith by someone who has been through the experience of Easter, who has been invaded by the spirit of Christ and can only speak of him in the light of his resurrection. The further question of where precisely such and such an event or word took place or was spoken, or when, or how, comes in second place.

And if this is true of the whole gospel narrative, it is especially true of its opening pages. Here above all the evangelist is asserting his faith, not writing a diary.

Does this mean that the Christmas stories have no biographical basis at all, that they might have been made up entirely out of the blue? Of course not. None but the most extreme sceptic would deny that a number of basic facts control the narrative and give it direction. In fact a comparison of the two stories in Matthew and Luke would suggest that, at the very least, those elements which are common to both are presumably historical facts : the persons of Jesus, Mary and Joseph; their descent from David; their home in Nazareth; the person of Herod. And it is interesting that these are precisely the historical details which occur in the gospel of John, and which therefore we would have known even if the Christmas stories had never been written.

But it needs repeating that these facts – and whatever others anyone would wish to establish – are pressed into service for a theological purpose, not a biographical one. The facts are used in the freest possible manner and re-thought in the light both of the Old Testament and of the resurrection. This means that it is often impossible for us, today, to tell which part of the narrative is biographical detail and which is theological reflection.

It means too that the accounts of Matthew and Luke cannot be harmonized. If two authors are writing independent *biographies,* then it is fair to try to interleave the two and show the extent to which they agree. But the stories in which two authors express their *theology* cannot be cut up and pieced together to form one coherent narrative, and it would be as pointless to do this as to try to make one composite picture of a Rembrandt and a Velasquez portrait of the same person. Each is a valid portrait, in its own right.

But perhaps we have sufficiently laboured the point, and sufficiently prepared ourselves for reading the Christmas stories in the spirit in which they were written. It is time we began to look at the stories in detail.

3. Jesus and the Old Testament
St Matthew's Approach

Since I have emphasized so strongly that Matthew and Luke are distinct theological reflections on the meaning of Jesus' life and death, not to be confused with each other and made into one story, it would seem best to devote a chapter to each. This will allow us to see more clearly the distinctive approach that each of them brings to his subject, and to ask the right question, which is not, 'What did Jesus mean when he . . .?' but 'What does the evangelist mean when he presents us with this story of Jesus?' This chapter will be devoted to the theology of Matthew.

POETRY AND MYTH

In describing above the kind of literature that the Christmas stories are, I made frequent use of the word 'poetry'. This is possibly a rather weak word for what we are trying to grasp here. So also is the word 'myth', which was frequently used by the first critical scholars of the infancy narratives to express the similarities they saw between these stories and the Greek hero legends. Some of the parallels they drew are valid up to a point, as we shall see later. But if 'myth' means simply a fabrication which cannot be taken seriously, then the word is inadequate and the judgement superficial.

An example might illustrate the point. I was recently reading a medieval legend from the Tyrol. It told of little Catholic children being kidnapped by Jews so that they could be murdered in one of the ritual services held in the synagogue. Horror stories were not invented in Hammersmith.

The Catholic writer who was quoting the legend called it 'a fantastic tissue of old wives' tales, complete with miracles and revelations'.

There is no one who will doubt that, at the level of literal history, this judgement is perfectly correct. The question is, would we apply the same criterion to the stories contained in the New Testament, and especially to the Christmas stories? If not, why not? If different standards are to be applied there, why?

In other words, the Catholic writer was saying : 'This story is full of revelations and miracles. These sort of things do not happen in everyday life. Therefore the story is a fabrication. It gives itself away. I refuse to accept it as a piece of history.'

The conclusion is right, *as far as it goes*. The trouble is that it does not go far enough. If we today can recognize a story as unhistorical, is it not reasonable to suppose that the person who composed it had at least as much insight? To say that it is unhistorical is only to specify what it is not. But what is it positively? What did the writer intend it to be?

In the case in question, the answer is fairly obvious. It is intended to be a piece of anti-Semitic writing. That at least is something concrete. That at least is something serious, which ought to be discussed and not just dismissed as 'unhistorical'. We must ask the right questions of a piece of literature.

ASKING THE RIGHT QUESTIONS

To apply this to the Christmas stories. If we ask only

historical questions, then we will arrive at conclusions which may be valid *as far as they go*, but perhaps we ought to go further. If it is clear that they are not a piece of literal description, is that any reason for dismissing them? Perhaps they were never intended to be read as a piece of literal description. Perhaps we are asking the wrong questions of the text. Perhaps we ought to begin asking different questions.

It has often been pointed out that the Christmas stories contain a number of elements common to much folk literature. The wicked king, oriental magicians, threats against the life of a child, supernatural protection, guidance by a star, messages from heaven – these details do not occur only in Matthew and Luke. What is to be concluded? That these sort of things do not happen and that therefore the stories are not worth our attention? Or that this is so obviously not a literal description of fact that the story must have some other purpose? We must ask the right questions of the text.

It is related of St Ambrose that, while he was still a child in his cot, a swarm of bees was discovered in his mouth. Only a fool would ask the date that this happened. This is a story about his honeyed eloquence, not a lesson in apiary. The orphaned child Romulus is said to have been miraculously preserved by being suckled by a she-wolf. Only a philistine would ask to be shown the spot. This is a story about a man destined by the gods for greatness, not a disquisition on mammals.

Anyone anxious to prove these stories untrue would have to show, not that these events never took place, but that Ambrose was not eloquent and that Romulus was not great. We have to ask where precisely the truth of the story lies. The truth of the story about the journey into Egypt is not proved by pointing to a tree outside Cairo. We must ask the right questions.

OLD TESTAMENT PROPHECIES?

This may seem a roundabout way of approaching the
opening chapters of St Matthew, but the point will
emerge after a closer look at the Old Testament texts
quoted in these chapters.

Anyone beginning to read St Matthew's gospel in a
translation which distinguishes clearly between the
author's own material and the quotations he is using, will
be struck by the fact that the first two chapters are punctuated with five clear quotations, each preceded by the
rubric : 'This took place in order to fulfil what the Old
Testament had foretold in the following words . . .' Anyone who took the pains to trace the texts quoted back
into the Old Testament would discover that none of
them are in fact predictions about the birth and childhood of Jesus. They all refer to something quite different.

BEHOLD A VIRGIN SHALL CONCEIVE

The text is from Isaiah 7. The context is the eighth century B.C., with the Assyrian troops massed on the
Israelite border, and the childless king of Jerusalem terrified that Israel will be overrun, and the sacred royal
line of David come to an end in his own death.

The prophet Isaiah is, on the one hand, angry with
the king for having so little faith in God's power to protect his people, and on the other trying to reassure him.
Such reassurance, in such a situation, is not likely to
take the form of a promise that God is going to do something wonderful in seven hundred years' time!

This is what he says :

Listen now, House of David :
are you not satisfied with trying the patience of men
without trying the patience of my God, too?
The Lord himself, therefore,
will give you a sign.
It is this : the Virgin is with child
and will soon give birth to a son
whom she will call Immanuel . . .
For before this child knows how to refuse evil
and choose good,
the land whose two kings terrify you
will be deserted.

Isaiah's words seem to refer to the 'Virgin Israel'
who, he assures the king, will not be raped by Assyria's
allies, but give birth to the child who will ensure the con-
tinuation of the royal line, and so prove that God has not
abandoned us but continues to be at our side. Immanu-el
means 'God is with us'. It is clear from the chapters that
follow that Isaiah hoped that the child referred to,
Hezekiah, would grow up and prove to be a second
David, the messiah that Israel hoped for. His hopes were
disappointed.

FROM YOU, BETHLEHEM, SHALL COME
A RULER

The text is from Micah 5. The context is the same
political crisis as that referred to by Isaiah, and it is
spoken of here in terms of Zion (Jerusalem) labouring in
birth-pangs.

To you, the fortified Sheepfold,
hill of the daughter of Zion,

shall be given back your former sovereignty . . .
Why are you crying out aloud . . .
that pains should grip you like a woman in labour?
Writhe, cry out, daughter of Zion . . .
Out of you, Bethlehem in Ephrathah,
though you are the least of the clans of Judah,
will be born one who is to rule over Israel,
one whose origin goes back to the distant past,
to the days of old.
The Lord will only abandon Israel
until the one who is with child gives birth . . .
He will stand and feed his flock
in the power of the Lord.

Micah too looks forward to a solution of the situation by
the birth of a better king than the one then in power.
Perhaps the next king would be another shepherd like
David, springing like him from the ancient Bethlehem
clan (whatever his actual birthplace, which is immaterial
to this hope).

Micah too was disappointed, and his hope for such a
shepherd-ruler remained unfulfilled in his lifetime.

OUT OF EGYPT HAVE I CALLED MY SON

The text is from Hosea 11, a fine poetic passage in
which God is pictured arguing with himself about how
best to deal with his wayward child, Israel. The way-
wardness is illustrated by recounting the history of
Israel :

When Israel was a child I loved him,
he was my son, and I called him out of Egypt.

Yet the more I called him
the further he wandered from me . . .
It was I who taught him how to walk,
it was I who took him in my arms . . .
I stooped down to give him his food . . .
So how could I ever abandon him?
I am his father; Israel is my son.

Hosea is expressing his faith that the bond which will
keep God indissolubly faithful to Israel was forged in the
Exodus from Egypt, when he freely chose Israel to become his son.

A VOICE IN RAMAH,
RACHEL WEEPING FOR HER CHILDREN

The text is from Jeremiah 31. It speaks of the situation
in the sixth century B.C., with Jerusalem destroyed and
Israel exiled into Assyria, and Judah into Babylonia.
The prophet Jeremiah, lamenting the disaster, but also
trying to give hope to the exiles, is reconstructing what
happened.

He remembers Ramah, the concentration camp north
of Jerusalem, where the deportees were collected before
their long march north. According to tradition, Ramah
was the burial place of Rachel, mother of the Joseph
tribes who made up the kingdom of Israel.

Thus speaks the Lord :
A voice is heard in Ramah,
lamenting and weeping bitterly :
it is Rachel weeping for her children
because they are no more.

But he goes on to assure her that her tears will turn into joy when the exiles return. The text from which Matthew is quoting continues with the words: 'Stop your weeping, dry your eyes . . . they shall come back.'

HE SHALL BE CALLED A NAZARENE

This 'quotation' does not in fact correspond to any text that can be found in the Old Testament. But it does correspond to a dedication service known as the 'nazirate'. By a personal vow or by a parent's promise, a man could be marked out for a period of time or for life as consecrated to God in a special way. One of the most famous *nazirs* dedicated to God by this ceremony was Samson. The word has nothing to do with the village of Nazareth, with which St Matthew connects the quotation.

What ought one to conclude from this short investigation into the original meaning of the Old Testament texts quoted by Matthew?

One could conclude that the whole thing is quite meaningless. Matthew has offered us five Old Testament prophecies of the future: the Virgin Birth, Bethlehem, the Flight into Egypt, the Slaughter of the Innocents, Nazareth. We have looked at them and discovered that none of them refer to the future. He cannot be serious. Why waste time on reading this sort of stuff? It's a lot of nonsense.

Alternatively, one could conclude that we were asking the wrong questions. Is it not possible, indeed likely, that he *was* serious, but that he was concerned with something entirely different from what we expected? Should we not look at his text more closely, and more deeply, and begin asking different questions?

THE GENEALOGY

The opening paragraph of Matthew is devoted to a genealogy of Jesus. This is perhaps as good a paragraph as any to tell us what kind of questions the author is inviting the reader to ask him, questions which have very little to do with history.

He begins with the words, 'A genealogy of Jesus Christ *son of David*.' It is worth remarking that the body of the gospel is itself very chary in its use of those words. 'Son of David' was in fact one of the titles given to the hoped-for messiah, suggestive of the role he was expected to play as king and liberator. As such it had political overtones with which it would seem Jesus did not wish to associate himself. Whenever, as the gospel story unfolds, this or a similar title is applied to him, he is said to be embarrassed by it to the extent that he either refuses the title or asks it to be kept secret. In fact these texts have made many scholars conclude that the claim to be messiah was never made by Jesus himself, only by his disciples after his death and resurrection. This would not mean that Jesus was not in fact messiah, only that he never spoke of his mission in those words.

In either case, whether he disclaimed the title altogether or only played it down for fear of the misunderstanding it could lead to, it is obvious that a genealogy showing his descent from king David was not something proudly preserved in Jesus' family in case he ever needed it later to prove his pedigree. It is clearly a Christian construction, an expression of the belief of Jesus' disciples that, despite all appearances to the contrary, he was the fulfilment of Jewish messianic hopes. They called him, as we do, the *mashiah* (Hebrew) or the *christos* (Greek), the one anointed or appointed by God.

In that context, we can appreciate the artificial character of the genealogy. For instance, two deliberate pauses are made to divide the otherwise uninterrupted list of names into three series of fourteen. It is done so deliberately that the author has to omit the names of four kings who would otherwise have featured in the list, and to use the name of Jechoniah twice. And in case any reader has not been observant enough to notice that each series does in fact contain fourteen names, he mentions the fact explicitly at the end of the genealogy. Why fourteen? It is possible that the author is making use of the 'gematry' popular in his time, by which symbolic significance is attributed to the sum total of a person's name, given the fact that letters were also used as numbers. In Hebrew the letters DVD add up to fourteen. The whole list of names points three times over to Jesus as a second David.

It is also just about possible that the symbolism of the sacred number seven, which represented totality and completion, was seen to lie behind all this, as it certainly does in many other places in scripture. In that case the three fourteens would represent six sevens, and Jesus would mark the beginning of the seventh seven, or the fullness of time.

The three series into which the list is artificially divided are headed by the names of Abraham, David, and the exile. Abraham was the father of the promise on which the whole Old Testament is based; David was the founder of the royal dynasty around which so many of Israel's hopes centred; the exile marked the beginning of Judaism as it existed in New Testament times. Three important turning points in the history of Israel, and each is made to focus attention on Jesus as the fulfilment of that promise and that dynasty, and the crown of Judaism.

Strangely, the list is not composed exclusively of stained glass royal ancestors, but includes an unforgettable sinner, the unfaithful Bathsheba (not to mention quite a number of kings who 'did that which is evil in the sight of the Lord'), and even two prominent gentiles who look strangely out of place in a Jewish pedigree, Rahab of Jericho and Ruth of Moab. Jesus is the descendant not only of a chosen race, but also of sinners and aliens.

If these are the theological concerns of the author, is there any point in asking questions about the historical reliability of the text, or in trying to reconcile it with the almost totally different genealogy of Luke, whose list of names from David to Jesus has only two names in common with Matthew's? Surely in both cases the genealogy is too partial and too artificial to allow us to answer such questions. More to the point, in both cases the genealogy, whatever its historical accuracy or inaccuracy, is not being used as a genealogy at all. It is a statement of faith in what Jesus means to the evangelist. And he issues that statement as an invitation to us to share his faith, so that we may come to know Jesus as he knows him.

Does that mean that the real genealogy of Jesus is unknown? Perhaps. Does it matter? Would it help anyone to know it?

THE BIBLE ACCORDING TO MATTHEW

It is significant that the word Matthew uses for genealogy is *genesis*. A strictly literal translation of his opening words would be, '*The book of Genesis* of Jesus Christ'. Rather like the fourth gospel, whose opening lines are a deliberate echo of the first page of Genesis, 'In the be-

ginning,' so Matthew is offering to retell the whole Old
Testament in the light of Jesus Christ.

More strictly his interest lies in that part of the Bible
which was attributed to Moses, the five-volumed Law or
Pentateuch. In fact the body of the gospel, in imitation
of the Pentateuch, is divided into five 'books' by the repetition of the same closing phrase ('When Jesus had
finished speaking these words . . .', Matthew 7 : 28, 11 : 1,
13 : 53, 19 : 1, 26 : 1) in order to present the teaching of
Jesus as the new Law bringing to perfection the word of
God contained in the old Law.

But in this introductory section, Matthew's scope is
wider. It is the whole of the Old Testament that he
wishes to cover in one sweep to show Jesus as the fulfilment of its deepest longings.

He does this by drawing attention to a number of explicit quotations, and making passing allusions to a host
of others, taken from books running the whole gamut of
the Old Testament. The explicit quotations have already
been referred to above. Our concern here is to look more
closely at the use Matthew has made of them. For the
sake of convenience we will take them, not in the order
Matthew quotes them, but in the historical order with
which we are more familiar.

MOSES THE SAVIOUR

The story of the return from Egypt opens with the
angel's assurance to Joseph that 'those who wanted to
kill the child are dead' (Matthew 2 : 20). Why 'those' in
the plural, when the story has spoken of only one,
Herod? Because the phrase has been borrowed from
Exodus 4 : 19 where Moses is urged to come out of his
desert exile and return to his brethren because 'those'
who were once out for his blood are now dead. The fact

that Matthew has turned back to the book of Exodus to borrow this phrase suggests that he is thinking of Jesus as a new Moses.

This throws light on the story immediately preceding, of the massacre of the innocents. The slaughter of children is precisely the means Pharaoh had used to try to eliminate a possible Moses. In the Exodus story, God had foiled this plan by intervening to spare the infant Mōses. Is this the material out of which the Herod story is constructed?

The suggestion is lent some colour by a comparison of the details in Matthew's story with the rabbinic elaborations or *midrashim* on the Exodus story of Moses. There the birth of Moses is foretold to his father in a dream, as Jesus' birth is foretold here to the dreaming Joseph. There Pharaoh is forewarned of the birth, as Herod is here of Jesus' birth. There all Egypt trembles at the news, as all Jerusalem does here. There Pharaoh consults astrologers for advice on what he should do, as Herod here consults the magi.

If Matthew's story is based on these texts, and it gives every indication that it is, then it means that we can no longer put our finger on the present reality underlying his story. All we can put our finger on is the past reality – the providence of God whereby Moses was raised up as a saviour of his people. And the only 'fact' about Jesus that Matthew would then be stating in this story is that Jesus is a new Moses.

THE JUDGE-LIBERATORS

And not only a new Moses, but also a new judge, if that is the right word for those leaders of Israel who took over the role of the dying Moses. The very last line of the infancy narrative is a reference to this period of Israelite history, by means of a 'quotation' which, as was pointed out above, is not a real quotation at all, but only a reference to a service of dedication or consecration known as the 'nazirate'. By a play of words, Matthew connects this with Nazareth.

The most famous *nazir* in Israelite history was Samson, and it is him whom Matthew seems to have in mind (as Luke quite explicitly does in his infancy narrative, see chapter 4 below) when he speaks of Jesus' birth in these words : 'The angel of the Lord appeared . . . and said . . . She has conceived . . . and will give birth to a son . . . he is the one who is to save his people . . . he will be called a Nazarene.' (Matthew 1 :20-1, 2 :23) This is a fairly close echo of the story of Samson whose birth is told in almost the same words : 'The angel of the Lord appeared . . . and said . . . You will conceive and bear a son . . . It is he who will begin to rescue Israel . . . the boy shall be God's *nazir*.' (Judges 13 :3-7)

So Jesus begins to appear as summing up not only the period of Israel's exodus from Egypt, but also the period of Israel's judges, those consecrated leaders who defended God's people against their oppressors and liberated them from their enemies.

KING AND KINGDOM

The period of the judges was followed by the experiment in monarchy which subsequently played such an important part in Israel's history and hopes. The two 'royal' texts which Matthew quotes from Isaiah and Micah ('A virgin shall conceive', 'From you, Bethlehem, shall come a ruler') have already been mentioned above. Both refer to the dynasty of David, and not only refer

back to the first David but explicitly look forward to a
second. In fact many of the Old Testament 'royal' texts,
even though they were originally written with an actual
historical person in mind, were later taken up to express
Israel's yearning for a king who would live up to the
hopes so often disappointed by the kings of its history.

The same 'royal' theme, which in any case was already
announced in the opening genealogy, as we have seen, is
alluded to in the title 'son of David' given to Joseph as
Jesus' genealogical father (Matthew 1 :20), and in the
question of the magi who ask where the 'king of the Jews'
is to be found (Matthew 2 :2).

Through these texts, then, Matthew is professing his
faith in Jesus as the son of David for whom the history
of Israel had longed. And not just any son of David, as
king Solomon was for instance. We are dealing with
someone greater than Solomon here, as will be stated
quite explicitly in the body of the gospel (see Matthew
12 :42), and as is intimated here in describing the homage paid to the infant with gold and spices from the east
in terms similar to those in which the queen of Sheba's
homage to Solomon is described in the Old Testament :
'She presented the king with . . . gold and great quan-
tities of spices . . . Then she went home, she and her
servants, to her own country.' (1 Kings 10 :10, 13) It is
interesting that Matthew has used the same signing-off
line to end his story of the magi.

A rabbinic *midrash* on this passage from the Old
Testament even mentions that the queen of Sheba was
guided to Solomon by a star. This suggests that some of
the scholarly 'explanations' of the star which led the
magi (a meteor, an appearance of Halley's comet in 12
B.C., a conjunction of Jupiter, Saturn and Mars in 7
B.C., the Holy Ghost taking on the form of a star, have
all been suggested) have been rather pointless; it is no

more than a detail borrowed from the Old Testament
tradition to express the faith that Jesus is not only a
new Moses and a new liberator, but a new Davidic king
greater than Solomon in all his glory.

Perhaps mention should also be made here of two
other Old Testament passages which seem to have influenced the telling of the story of the magi : the hopes
expressed in the book of Isaiah for a restoration of
Jerusalem's faded glory :

> Arise, shine out, for your light has come . . .
> kings will come to your dawning brightness . . .
> the wealth of the nations will come to you;
> camels in throngs will cover you,
> and dromedaries of Midian and Ephah;
> everyone in Sheba will come,
> bringing gold and incense   (Isaiah 60 : 1, 3, 5, 6)

and the psalmist's vision of the ideal king of the future :

> The kings of Tarshish and of the islands
> will pay him tribute.
> The kings of Sheba and Seba
> will offer gifts . . .
> may gold from Sheba be given him!
>
> (Psalm 72 : 10, 15a)

It is significant that this last prayer has a title dedicating
it to king Solomon.

RESTORATION

The Israelite experiment in monarchy ended when the
populations of both kingdoms, kings included, were
exiled, some to Assyria and the rest to Babylonia. This

period of Old Testament history is recalled by Matthew
in his reference to Rachel weeping for her children – the
northern tribes exiled into the wilderness, with apparently no hope of return. But the page of the Old
Testament from which the quotation is taken is not as
pessimistic as the isolated quotation would suggest; it
is heavy with the promise of restoration:

They have found pardon in the wilderness . . .
I have loved you with an everlasting love . . .
Proclaim! Praise! Shout:
'The Lord has saved his people' . . .
See, I will bring them back
from the land of the North . . .
I will comfort them as I lead them back . . .
For I am a father to Israel,
he is my first-born son . . .
A voice is heard in Ramah,
lamenting and weeping bitterly:
it is Rachel weeping for her children
because they are no more.
But the Lord says this:
Stop your weeping,
dry your eyes . . .
they shall come back from the enemy country . . .
For the Lord is creating something new on earth:
the Woman sets out to find her Husband again . . .
I will make a new covenant with the House of Israel,
but not like the one I made with their ancestors
on the day I took them by the hand to bring them out
    of the land of Egypt . . .
this is the covenant I will make with the House of
    Israel . . .
Deep within them I will plant my Law, writing it on
    their hearts.

Then I will be their God and they shall be my people.

(Jeremiah 31 :2-33)

It is clear that Jeremiah looked forward to the return from exile as a kind of second exodus, as a repetition of that foundational experience in which Israel was first created and saved, and understood itself to be both a son and a bride of God, bound to him by an everlasting covenant. In this context it is significant that Matthew puts the quotation from Jeremiah right next to his explicit reference to the first exodus when Israel was first called out of Egypt to become son of God (Matthew 1 :15=Hosea 11 :1).

In short, Matthew sees the birth and infancy of Jesus as the culmination of those two great exoduses of the Old Testament, the presage of that final Exodus which would mark the complete restoration of God's people.

JESUS AND THE OLD TESTAMENT

We could sum up Matthew's profession of faith in something like these words : 'The whole history of the Old Testament flows together in Jesus, from Moses and the exodus, through the judges and the splendour of the kingdom and the wisdom of Solomon, down to the exile and the hope of restoration. The texts I have chosen to suggest this are not simple foretellings of the future, but something much deeper – an evocation of the Old Testament's most important themes : Passover, Liberation, Exile, Restoration, Kingdom of God. It is in the light of those themes that I want you to see Jesus. He is the messiah, not because he was predicted in a few scattered texts – that would scarcely do him justice – but because he is the fulfilment of all that the Old Testament had been searching for, and the meaning behind all its questioning.'

We were asking above whether the quoting of apparently random texts, which seem at first sight to have nothing to do with the New Testament, could possibly be taken seriously. The purpose of this chapter has been to show how deceptive first sight can be. The use Matthew has made of the Old Testament is the most serious thing in the world. He has shown what a truly Christian reading of the Old Testament can be.

If we ask what precise historical events these two chapters of Matthew have been based on, we can only answer that we do not know, and that when we are dealing with a theology as dense as this, that sort of question sounds singularly inappropriate.

Or better, we can answer that *the* historical event on which these two chapters are based is the death and resurrection of Jesus. The sky doing extraordinary things to point to the uniqueness of this person, the whole of Jerusalem trembling at the news, Herod and his official advisers laying about them in their determination to do away with him – these are not anticipations of the death and resurrection, a kind of preview of it thirty years beforehand. It is the other way round. Jesus' death and resurrection took place first, before these stories were written. The stories are an echo of that event, not a foretaste of it.

It is in Jesus' death and resurrection that Matthew discovered Jesus to be the new Moses rescuing his people from slavery, the new David bringing about the kingdom of God on earth, the new Solomon in all his glory, the new Israel rising out of the ashes of the old. It was the facts of Jesus' life and death, not of his birth, which justified such a theology.

4. Jesus and the Old Testament
St Luke's Approach

I mentioned above that I have deliberately chosen to deal with Luke's infancy narratives separately from those of Matthew in order to emphasize that each of the evangelists presents his own theology, standing in its own right.

If what they had presented was straightforward history, then one would naturally want to deal with both accounts together, and expect one to give supplementary information to fill out the other. And if this were the situation, it would be the duty of the commentator to show the connection between the two accounts, to interleave them and try to harmonize them. But not only is there almost nothing in Luke which can be woven into the existing Matthew; even the little there seems to be only produces a tangle.

To explain. The only details Luke has in common with Matthew are three names (Jesus, Mary and Joseph), three places (Jerusalem, Bethlehem and Nazareth), and the time (Herod the Great, therefore before 4 B.C.). All the rest that he has to offer is new.

Should one therefore treat Luke's material as 'supplementary information' to be woven into Matthew's account as best one can? One only has to try it to see how difficult this is. For instance, according to Matthew, after Jesus' birth in Bethlehem, Mary and Joseph proceed directly to Egypt where they stay until the death

of Herod, and then, avoiding Judea, they make their
way to Nazareth. According to Luke, after Jesus' birth in
Bethlehem, Mary and Joseph proceed to the temple in
Jerusalem, and from there make their way straight to
Nazareth. In other words, in Luke's account there is no
room for any visit to Egypt; and in Matthew's there is
no room for any presentation in the Jerusalem temple.
The two stories can only be made into one by tying
oneself into a knot.

The tangle disappears as soon as we realize that we
are not dealing with two chronicles or diaries of observ-
able events, but with two theologies or meditations on
the Old Testament. And if Luke has chosen different
Old Testament texts to meditate on, there is no reason
why his narrative should coincide or interleave with
Matthew's.

WHERE HAVE I HEARD THAT BEFORE?

The contents of Luke's infancy narrative are familiar to
anyone who has ever used a rosary; its sections have provided the names for the five joyful 'mysteries' or meditation points of which the rosary is composed : the Annunciation, the Visitation, the Nativity, the Presentation,
the Finding in the Temple. Indeed, it would be difficult
to conceive of five joyful 'mysteries' named after Matthew's narrative : the Genealogy, the Visit of the Magi,
the Flight into Egypt, the Massacre of the Innocents,
the Retirement into Nazareth !

The rosary is based on the second chapter of Luke.
Indeed for most people the words 'annunciation, nativity,
circumcision' will immediately make them think of what
is there said of Jesus. What it ought to make them think
is, 'Where have I heard that before?' Because Luke tells

not simply of one annunciation-nativity-circumcision, but of two, and the series in the second chapter is meant to be seen in the light of the series in the first chapter, which tells of John the Baptist.

In other words, Luke deliberately places the infancy narrative of Jesus in strict parallel to his infancy narrative of the Baptist. The coming of both is announced by the angel Gabriel. The birth of both is described, and the circumcision, and the naming ceremony, and the hidden life. In fact, to make sure that the parallelism is recognized by the reader, Luke uses similar phrases to conclude the two stories : '(John) grew up and his spirit matured', 1 :80 = 'Jesus increased in wisdom and stature, 2 :52; 'The hand of the Lord was with (John)', 1 :66 = 'Jesus increased . . . in favour with God', 2 :52.

A detailed comparison of the two accounts will show how close this parallelism can be at times :

The Annunciation to Zechariah	*The Annunciation to Mary*
Zechariah and Elizabeth	Joseph and Mary
Enter the angel Gabriel	Enter the angel Gabriel
Zechariah is disturbed	Mary is deeply disturbed
'Do not be afraid'	'Do not be afraid'
'Elizabeth is to bear a son'	'You are to bear a son'
'You must name him John'	'You must name him Jesus'
'He will be great'	'He will be great'
His task is described	His task is described
'How can I be sure?'	'How can this be?'
A sign is given	A sign is given

LUKE THE ARTIST

By long tradition, St Luke has been accorded the title of artist. The word is usually taken to refer to pictorial artistry, and representations of St Luke often show him

with a paint-brush in his hand. But it is possible that
the tradition refers to his literary artistry, his skill with
the pen. Certainly in the dedicatory preface with which
he opens his gospel he says that his declared aim is to
write an 'orderly' account (Luke 1 :3), and the body of
the gospel bears this out. Where Mark and Matthew
have often incorporated material in a rather haphazard
fashion, Luke has a feeling for order which gives it shape
and symmetry. The same is true, to an even greater extent, of the independent material he has collected on his
own account for incorporation into his gospel.

So it is here, in the infancy narratives with which he
has decided to introduce the gospel story. The balance
and the harmony betray the artist's hand. Luke wants
his readers to appreciate the parallelism between John
the Baptist and Jesus in order to understand how much
the latter towers over the former. These two chapters
are, in effect, a literary elaboration of the statement of
John the Baptist with which the main body of the gospel
begins : 'One is coming after me who is mightier than
me.' (Luke 3 :16)

WHERE HAVE I HEARD THAT BEFORE?

But even when the reader has realized that, he is still
not finished. He is being invited to ask again, 'Now,
where have I heard that before?' Because even the story
of John the Baptist is not the first draft; it is itself a
copy. For the original we must turn to 1 Samuel, which
like Matthew and Luke devotes its opening two chapters
to an infancy narrative :

(Elkanah) had two wives, one called Hannah, the

other Peninnah; Peninnah had children but Hannah had none . . . the Lord had made her barren . . . In the bitterness of her soul she prayed to the Lord with many tears and made a vow, saying, 'Lord of hosts! If you will take notice of the distress of your servant, and bear me in mind and not forget your servant and give her a man-child, I will give him to the Lord for the whole of his life and no razor shall ever touch his head' . . . Eli answered her : 'Go in peace,' he said 'and may the God of Israel grant what you have asked of him'. And she said, 'May your maidservant find favour in your sight' . . . and the Lord was mindful of her. She conceived and gave birth to a son, and called him Samuel 'since' she said 'I asked the Lord for him' . . . When she had weaned him . . . she brought him to the temple of the Lord . . . Then Hannah said this prayer :

My heart exults in the Lord . . .
for I rejoice in your power of saving.
There is none as holy as the Lord . . .
The bow of the mighty is broken
but the feeble have girded themselves with
    strength . . .
the famished cease from labour . . .
The Lord makes poor and rich,
he humbles and also exalts.
He raises the poor from the dust,
he lifts the needy from the dunghill
to give them a place with princes . . .
he endows his king with power,
he exalts the horn of his Anointed . . .

Meanwhile the boy Samuel grew up in the presence of the Lord . . . (He) went on growing in stature and

in favour both with the Lord and with men. (1 Samuel
1 :2 — 2 :26)

No one familiar with Luke's infancy narrative could
fail to hear the overtones of it that are contained in this
story : the mother's barrenness, the assurance from
heaven that she is to give birth, the consecration from
birth, the naming, the *Magnificat* of praise, the presentation in the Temple, the growth in favour with God and
men. No one coming to these Old Testament chapters
straight from Luke could fail to recognize how heavily
he has relied on them for his own infancy narrative.

And even at that point, anyone whose ear is well at-
tuned to the Old Testament would still have to say to
himself, 'Now, where have I heard that before?' Because even the story of Samuel is itself an echo of a whole
number of other annunciation and nativity stories. The
same theme is easily recognizable in the stories of Isaac,

The Lord dealt kindly with Sarah as he had said, and
did what he had promised her. So Sarah conceived
and bore a son to Abraham in his old age, at the time
God had promised. Abraham named the son born to
him Isaac, the son to whom Sarah had given birth.
Abraham circumcized his son Isaac when he was eight
days old, as God had commanded him. Abraham was
a hundred years old when his son Isaac was born to
him. Then Sarah said, 'God has given me cause to
laugh; all those who hear of it will laugh with me . . .
I have borne him a child in his old age' (Genesis
21 :1-7)

and of Gideon,

The angel of the Lord appeared to (Gideon) and said,

'The Lord is with you, valiant warrior!' Gideon answered him, 'Forgive me, my lord, but if the Lord is with us, then why is it that all this is happening to us now?' . . . The Lord answered him, 'I will be with you' . . . Gideon said to him, 'If I have found favour in your sight, give me a sign that it is you who speak to me' (Judges 6 : 12-17)

and of Samson

(Manoah's) wife was barren, she had borne no children. The angel of the Lord appeared to this woman and said to her, 'You are barren and have had no child. But from now on take great care. Take no wine or strong drink, and eat nothing unclean. For you will conceive and bear a son. No razor is to touch his head, for the boy shall be God's nazirite from his mother's womb. It is he who will begin to rescue Israel.' (Judges 13 : 2-5)

The theme common to all these stories is that of Israel's leaders as the gift of God. Salvation does not come to mankind solely through men's efforts or endeavours, through merely human capacities or potentialities. It is always a creation of God, a Godsend from the one who transcends the best efforts of men. Salvation is always utterly of God. It is this theme which is in the mind of the author of 1 Samuel when he borrows the vocabulary of these stories, and in the mind of Luke when he echoes the words of 1 Samuel in order to speak of Jesus. We will need to come back to the theme again later in chapter 6 when we consider the story of Jesus' virgin birth.

INFANCY STORIES AND MARY

If anyone was interested to go further – not backwards, because we have gone just about as far as we can, but forwards – in order to find the same theme echoed in later stories, he would look in the apocryphal gospels which offer to tell us about the infancy of Mary, the mother of Jesus. He would find exactly the same tune being played : a childless woman named Hannah or Ann (her husband's name Joachim is apparently bor-rowed from another Anna, the Susanna of Daniel 13) is the reproach of her neighbours for her barrenness; she prays and heaven answers her plea in the gift of a child named Mary; the child is dedicated to God from birth, and is brought up in the sanctuary.

How much are these details worth? As history very little : they have all been borrowed. But as a theme, very much. Mary too is to be seen as one of the leaders of Israel, and as such she too is of God, a Godsend.

SENSE OF CLIMAX

Within this general theme of God-given leadership, Luke has something more specific in mind. For if he has based his treatment of Jesus' infancy not merely on Old Test-ament annunciation stories in general, but on the Samuel story in particular, it is in order to provide a sense of climax. Samuel marked the beginning of the line of prophets, and John the Baptist the end, for 'the law and the prophets were *until* John' (Luke 16 : 16); it is Jesus who is the purpose for which the whole institution of prophetism existed. Samuel was the anointer of David as

king in Bethlehem; John is the anointer of Jesus as the
new David, on whom the heavenly blessing is pro-
nounced : 'You are my Son, the beloved; my favour
rests on *you*' (Luke 3 :22). Samuel is born of a mother
who has had no children, and John the Baptist is born
of parents who are beyond the age of childbearing; Jesus
is born of a virgin. The sense of climax is unmistakable.
One can only admire the artistry with which it has been
achieved.

LUKE'S ALLUSIONS

This general framework within which Luke has constructed his Christmas stories already governs their meaning. Since he has based them so deliberately on the
Samuel stories, it is no longer possible to tell which details are taken from reality and which are simply echoes
from the Old Testament. Luke's meaning is to be sought
not at the level of history but at the level of the theological themes outlined above.

But this does not exhaust Luke's meaning. Within the
general framework he has, like Matthew, meditated
deeply on other Old Testament texts. Matthew has expressed his meditation through a number of explicit quotations of texts 'spoken by the Lord through the prophet'.
Luke has no quotations to which he draws the reader's
attention. He has instead a wealth of allusions whose
overtones will be heard by anyone who is familiar with
the Old Testament, or at least has a translation which
provides him with the necessary marginal cross-refer-
ences. We should examine the more obvious of these
allusions, in the order in which Luke has made them, to
understand something of his thought.

REDEMPTION

Luke's story of Zechariah's prayer :

> (Zechariah) was exercising his priestly office before
> God . . . and entered the Lord's sanctuary to burn
> incense there . . . Then there appeared to him the
> angel of the Lord, standing on the right of the altar
> of incense . . . The angel said to him . . . 'I am Gabriel
> who stand in God's presence, and I have been sent
> to speak to you and bring you this good news' (Luke
> 1 :8-11, 19)

is an echo of the prayer of Daniel pleading with God to
send redemption to his people :

> I (Daniel) was still speaking, still at prayer, confessing
> . . . the sins of my people Israel and placing my plea
> before the Lord my God . . . when Gabriel . . . flew
> suddenly down to me at the hour of the evening sacri-
> fice. He said to me . . . 'Seventy weeks are decreed . . .
> for introducing everlasting integrity . . . to the coming
> of an anointed Prince.' (Daniel 9 :20-5)

The reference is, in effect, a profession of faith that Jesus
is the redemption yearned for by the Old Testament.

DAY OF THE LORD

The description of John the Baptist in terms of Elijah :

> He will bring back many of the sons of Israel to the

Lord their God. With the spirit and power of Elijah,
he will go before him to turn the hearts of fathers towards their children and the disobedient back to the
wisdom that the virtuous have, preparing for the Lord
a people fit for him (Luke 1 : 16-17)

is an allusion to the final pages of the Old Testament :

I am going to send you Elijah the prophet before my
day comes, that great and terrible day. He shall turn
the hearts of fathers towards their children. (Malachi
3 : 23-4)

In other words, John's ministry of conversion is only a
preparation for Jesus, and the ministry of Jesus will be
the Day of the Lord.

THE COMING OF GOD

The greeting issued to Mary, and the response it evokes :

Rejoice, so highly favoured!
The Lord is with you . . .
Mary, do not be afraid;
you have won God's favour.
You are to conceive in the womb and bear a son . . .
The Almighty has done great things for me (Luke
1 : 28-31, 49)

is very closely dependent on a number of prophetical
texts :

Rejoice heart and soul, daughter of Zion!
Shout with gladness, daughter of Jerusalem!

See now, your king comes to you (Zechariah 9 :9)

Do not be afraid, be glad, rejoice,
for the Lord has done great things . . .
Sons of Zion, be glad,
rejoice in the Lord your God (Joel 2 :21, 23)

Shout for joy, daughter of Zion,
Israel, shout aloud !
Rejoice, exult with all your heart,
daughter of Jerusalem ! . . .
The Lord, the king of Israel, is in your midst (womb);
you have no more evil to fear . . .
Zion, have no fear . . .
The Lord your God is in your midst (womb),
a victorious warrior.
He will exult with joy over you,
he will renew you by his love;
he will dance with shouts of joy for you
as on a day of festival. (Zephaniah 3 :14-17)

The prophetical hope of a God who is no longer distant
and remote but in the midst, in the very womb, of his
people – that, Luke is intimating, is fulfilled in the birth
of Jesus.

THE PRESENCE OF GOD

The promise made to Mary :

The Holy Spirit will come upon you
And the power of the Most High
will cover you with its shadow (Luke 1 :35)

is an echo of a whole number of texts in the story of the

Exodus, where 'to cover with its shadow' is a technical term used of the traditional Cloud which expressed the presence of God in this desert episode, guiding the people on their journey, resting at their stopping-places, and manifesting itself particularly in the sacred tabernacle:

> The Cloud covered the mountain, and the glory of the Lord settled on the mountain of Sinai; for six days the Cloud covered it, and on the seventh day the Lord called to Moses from inside the Cloud. (Exodus 24 : 16)

> Moses could not enter the Tent of Meeting because of the Cloud that rested on it and because of the glory of the Lord that filled the tabernacle. (Exodus 40 :35)

> The people remained encamped as long as the Cloud rested on the tabernacle . . . however long the Cloud stayed above the tabernacle, the sons of Israel remained in camp in the same place, and when it lifted they set out. (Numbers 9 : 18-22)

Mary is being spoken of in this passage as the meeting place where men come into the presence of God.

ARK OF THE COVENANT

The account of Mary's visit to Elizabeth:

> As soon as Elizabeth heard Mary's greeting, the child leapt in her womb and Elizabeth was filled with the Holy Spirit. She . . . said . . . 'Why should I be honoured with a visit from the mother of my Lord? For the moment your greeting reached my ears, the child in my womb leapt for joy . . .' Mary stayed with

Elizabeth about three months (Luke 1 :41, 43, 56)

is deliberately based upon the story of the Ark of the
Covenant, symbolic of God's presence, and the blessing
and joy it brought to God's people :

> David and all the House of Israel danced before the
> Lord with all their might . . . David went in fear of
> the Lord that day. 'However can the Ark of the Lord
> come to me?' he said . . . The Ark of the Lord re-
> mained in the house of Obed-edom of Gath for three
> months, and the Lord blessed Obed-edom and his
> whole family . . . David . . . brought the Ark of God
> up from Obed-edom's house to the citadel of David
> with great rejoicing . . . And David danced . . . before
> the Lord with all his might. (2 Samuel 6 :5-14)

The presence of God is something that can only be
greeted with awe or with exultation. Luke is not inviting
us to ask gynaecological questions about Elizabeth's condition, only to appreciate the fact that Jesus is that presence of God, and Mary is the Ark which brings him into
our midst.

POVERTY

Mary's own song of exultation contains the lines :

> He has looked upon his lowly handmaid . . .
> He has pulled down princes from their thrones
> and exalted the lowly.
> The hungry he has filled with good things,
> the rich sent empty away. (Luke 1 :48-53)

Some of these lines, as we have seen above, are a direct quotation from the Song of Hannah. But the theme of poverty they embody is not confined to that one passage; it runs throughout the latter part of the Old Testament where poverty is seen not simply as an economic fact, but as the essential condition for knowing God as he really is. The poor or *anawim* are those who can no longer rely on their own resources – they have none – but can only throw themselves on the goodness of God. The prophets and psalmists make much of this theme : a glance at a concordance will indicate the extent to which they are preoccupied with the spirit of poverty.

Of the New Testament writers, it is Luke who places most emphasis on this theme. It is not surprising, therefore, that his two opening chapters are punctuated with poor people. Not only Mary, but Joseph, Zechariah, Elizabeth, Simeon, Anna, and the shepherds – these sum up a whole procession of Old Testament figures who knew that before God they were beggars.

And the most outstanding of all these is Jesus, the Son of Man who had 'nowhere to lay his head' (Luke 9 :58). When he is presented here as being born in another man's stable, it is simply an echo of the fact that, at the other end of his life, he was buried in another man's tomb. He is the supremely homeless one, the wanderer always on the move to the Jerusalem that lies beyond, because there alone will he be truly at home, in the house of his Father. The theme fascinates Luke throughout his gospel. These lines are the first hint of it.

THE TEMPLE

When John the Baptist's role is specified in the *Benedictus* sung by Zechariah :

You shall be called Prophet of the Most High,
for you will go before the Lord
to prepare the way for him
to give his people knowledge of salvation . . .
this by the tender mercy of our God
who from on high will bring the rising Sun to visit us.
(Luke 1 :76-8)

Luke has again turned to the passage from Malachi to
which he has already referred, only now it is to identify
the coming of God not only with the ministry of Jesus,
but with the person of Jesus :

I am going to send my messenger to prepare a way
before me. And the Lord you are seeking will suddenly
enter his temple . . . Who will be able to resist the
Day of his coming? . . . I mean to visit you for the
Judgement . . . No need for you to be afraid of me,
says the Lord of hosts . . . For you who fear my name,
the Sun of righteousness will shine out with healing in
its rays. (Malachi 3 :1-5, 20)

When Jesus came to the temple, Judgement Day had
come. But here we have already entered the next theme,
that of Jerusalem.

JERUSALEM

St Luke shows a profound interest in Jerusalem. The
second half of his gospel comprises one long journey to
Jerusalem. It is not simply that his account of Jesus'
public life ends there – the accounts of Matthew, Mark
and John do that too – but that the attention of the
reader is drawn to the theme from as early as the ninth

chapter with the announcement that 'the time drew near for him to be taken up, and he set his face towards Jerusalem' (Luke 9:51); and from then on the narrative is punctuated with the word Jerusalem as if with signposts. (See 9:53, 13:22, 13:33, 17:11, 18:31, 19:11, 19:28.) Jesus' life, he is saying, was really one long journey, a passing over from his life among men to the true home where he would be with his Father. And the climax of it took place where salvation had always taken place – in Jerusalem.

That emphasis on Jerusalem in the body of the gospel is echoed in the infancy stories here under discussion, which also come to a climax in Jerusalem, with the boy Jesus making his *bar-mitzvah* pilgrimage to the temple to become a 'son of the law'. And it is there that Luke puts on to his lips the mysterious words, 'Did you not know that I must be in my Father's house?' (Luke 2:49) Why look for him anywhere else? Where else would one expect to find him? The only place where he may be truly discovered is where his life finds its deepest meaning, in the Jerusalem where salvation takes place.

Nor does the theme come to an end with the gospel. Luke planned his gospel in two volumes, the second of which is now called the Acts of the Apostles, and this places exactly the same emphasis on Jerusalem. It is there that the resurrection appearances take place and the risen Christ gives his disciples their commission (Matthew and Mark had placed these events in Galilee). It is there that the orphaned disciples gather in the upper room, apparently too shattered even to move. It is there that the pentecostal experience promised on the opening page of the gospel takes place, to transform the frightened disciples into fishers of men.

Because now Jerusalem has become the point of departure for an even longer journey, the starting point for a much wider field of action. And the story of Acts is the story of the gradual dispersion of the Christian community from Jerusalem to the rest of Judæa, to the coast, to Samaria, to Antioch, to Asia Minor, to Greece, until in the last chapter they reach Rome.

ROME

Just as Jerusalem is symbolic for Luke, so is Rome. Rome was the capital of the Empire, and therefore the centre of the world. Once the word of God had been preached there, it had in principle already been spread throughout the known world. The gospel of Jesus Christ is not destined for a privileged few, it is for everyone. Of all the evangelists, Luke is the most universalist in outlook.

That universalist role of Rome finds its place in Luke's infancy stories too. Matthew had introduced the village of Bethlehem under the rubric, 'That is where the second David comes from, like the first.' Luke introduces it under the rubric, 'That is where Rome decreed that Jesus should be born.' (see Luke 2 : 1) The birth he is talking of is not an event in an obscure village of the Middle East, even in a village which had great significance for Jews. It is an event with worldwide repercussions.

'Jerusalem and Rome : A Tale of Two Cities' would make a good title for Luke's two-volumed gospel. His infancy narrative announces the theme on the opening page.

LUKE AND JOHN

It has often been pointed out that, of the first three gospels, it is that of Luke which is closest in feeling and in outlook to the fourth gospel. The short analysis which has been made above will indicate how well founded this judgement is. The themes Luke has chosen to elaborate are precisely the ones which any theology of John would list.

John, like Luke, places strong emphasis on the divinity of Christ : in fact, he attributes to Jesus titles more explicitly divine than can be found anywhere else in the New Testament, especially the sacred name 'I Am.' John like Luke regularly speaks of Jesus' life and deeds as bringing the very 'Glory' of God (Luke thought of it as the 'Cloud') into the world. For John as for Luke Jesus is the 'tabernacling' of God in our midst; by a play on words he even reproduces in Greek (skéné) the technical Hebrew word for God's presence among his people – the Shekinah (John 1 :14). For John as for Luke, Jesus is the Ark and Temple of God : his telling of the cleansing of the temple makes it clear that for him the Spirit of the risen Christ has come to replace the building in Jerusalem (John 2 :21, 4 :23). John speaks of Jesus' life, as Luke does, as a passover-journey : he conveys this exquisitely in the structure of his prologue, which is designed to show Jesus' life as a coming from and a return to the Father (John 1 :1-18), and the theme is found again in his explicit reference to Jesus' death as a passover (John 13 :1) and his association of Jesus with the passover-lamb (John 1 :29, 19 :36). John like Luke gives prominence to Jerusalem : it is there not in Galilee that Jesus' ministry is mainly conducted, and (as in Luke) the resurrection appearances take place. (The Galilee stories in John 21 are explicitly acknowledged to be an appendix to the gospel.) John like Luke is interested in the part played by the mother of Jesus in the scheme of things : he refers to her on his opening and on his closing pages as the Woman in whom the long work of purifying Israel for the coming of God is completed. (John 2 :4, 19 :26)

It used to be the fashion to say that John, writing as late as he did, must have been dependent on Luke for these theological insights. Now it is recognized that, however late the gospel of John was written, it incorporates material older than is contained in some passages of Matthew, Mark and Luke (see especially C. H. Dodd in his *Historical Tradition in the Fourth Gospel*, Cambridge, University Press, 1963). Is it not possible that Luke's profound meditation on the meaning of Jesus' life may depend on that of John?

LOSS OR GAIN?

It is time to come to some final conclusion about the Christmas stories as they have been told us by Matthew and Luke. Enough has now been said to indicate that, in a theology as rich as this, biographical questions ('How many magi were there?' 'How exactly did the star work?' 'How much of this conversation did Mary understand?' 'How did the child feel when he lost his parents?' 'What was Luke's source of information?' etc.) may be asked, but they cannot be answered, because the evangelists were concerned with something quite different. In fact to put biographical questions of this kind may lead to the trivialization of something which is quite obviously meant to provoke us to ask far deeper questions.

This should console those who fear that the approach to the Christmas stories here adopted may make them lose something irreplaceable. It has been the purpose of the preceding chapters to show that what they have lost has been replaced by something much more worthwhile. These stories were not told to make children goggle in amazement. They were told to embody a theological meditation as profound as the mystery of the resurrection itself, because they are rooted in the resurrection. They were told to give us an insight into the deepest meaning of the Old Testament, which all flows together in Christ, and into the deepest meaning of the New Testament, which needs the Old Testament to reveal its hidden depths.

5. The Childhood of Jesus in Fiction

I referred above in chapter 2 to the numerous 'apocryphal' stories about Jesus' birth and childhood which grew up in the early Church in the wake of the gospels, from the second century onwards. Since these were originally written for popular consumption and not merely for the delight of scholars (though it must be acknowledged that they have done invaluable critical work in translating, editing, analysing, dating and publishing them) I thought it would be useful to reproduce some excerpts from them here. Not, let me hasten to add, to suggest that any real comparison can be made between them and the gospel stories. Indeed, one of the purposes of publishing them here is to allow the contrast between the two to stand out.

There are obviously similarities which need to be recognized, and these will appear more readily to those who have not got an *idée fixe* about what is to be taken as 'gospel'. Dealing as they do with Jesus' 'hidden' life, these stories, like those in the gospel, have little or nothing in the way of hard facts to go on, and must rely on symbolism and poetry, inventiveness and imagination, often with great effect and beauty. There is the same emphasis on the supernatural, the marvellous and the miraculous. There is, at least at times, the same underlying theological interest – to emphasize the divinity of Christ, or to re-assert the fullness of his humanity when this seems to be becoming compromised, or to counter attacks on the faith of the community about the virgin birth, etc.

But alongside these similarities no honest reader can fail to be struck by the overall contrast in tone between these stories and those in the gospels of Matthew and Luke. These are no longer meditations on Old Testament texts : the Old Testament is barely referred to, and once in fact is expressly and venomously repudiated. These are no longer reflections on the meaning of Christ's risen life : some of the miracles recounted are bizarre in the extreme, and many are no more than playful pranks. The stories tend to fall into the category of pious fiction, designed to entertain and occasionally to edify.

This is not said to dismiss them. There is always room for edifying stories, and each age will invent the form of entertainment it finds most appropriate. The influence these stories exercised on medieval art is an indication of the need they filled. But apart from some rare exceptions these infancy stories lack that awe, seriousness and theological depth which, whatever is said about their historical value, will always make the stories of Matthew and Luke 'true' in a much more profound sense.

Those who, having sampled these excerpts, wish to delve further into this fascinating mine of stories will find as complete a text and commentary as they can reasonably hope for in the works of James and Hennecke[1]. My own indebtedness to them will be obvious to anyone who has consulted them.

From *The Birth of Mary* (no longer extant, but quoted

[1] M. R. James, *The Apocryphal New Testament*, Oxford University Press, 1924.

E. Hennecke, *New Testament Apocrypha*, 2 vols., English trans. ed. by R. M. Wilson, Lutterworth Press, London, 1963-5.

in the fourth century by Epiphanius, *Panarion*, 26, 12).
The vision which John the Baptist's father Zechariah
had in the temple struck him dumb, because what he
saw was a man in the form of an ass. This is why the
temple-priests were instructed to wear bells on their
vestments, so that this creature could hear them coming
and hide himself. When his speech finally returned and
he was able to tell the people what it was they had been
worshipping, they killed him.[2]

From *The Gospel according to the Hebrews* (no longer
extant, but quoted in a sermon in Coptic attributed to
Cyril of Jerusalem, fourth century).
When Christ wished to come among men on earth, God
the Father summoned a mighty Power in heaven called
Michael, and entrusted Christ to his care. This Power
came into the world under the name of Mary. After
Christ had been in her womb seven months, she gave
birth to him.

From *The Protogospel of James* (second century original
in Greek).
(18, 1) He (Joseph) found a cave and brought her (Mary)
into it, and leaving her in the care of his sons went

---

[2] Epiphanius, quoting this extraordinary story, is anxious to
repudiate it as 'horrible and destructive', recognizing it is a
vicious piece of anti-Old Testament propaganda for which the
Gnostics of the second century were famous. In the third
century Origen, like Epiphanius mistaking John the Baptist's
father for the Zechariah mentioned in Matthew 23:35, gives
another explanation of his death: he was murdered for con-
tinuing to allow Mary to take her place among the temple-
virgins, even after the birth of Jesus. The *Protogospel of James*
(see below) more straightforwardly attributes the murder to
Herod, infuriated that his child John had escaped the Bethlehem
massacre.

out to look for a Hebrew midwife around Bethlehem. (19, 1) He found one just coming down from the hill-country, who asked him, 'Who is the woman giving birth in the cave?' He said, 'My betrothed.' She asked him, 'Is she not your wife?', and he told her, 'She is Mary; she was brought up in the temple, and I was given her as wife by lot. But she is not my wife : she has conceived by the Holy Spirit.' The midwife said to him, 'Is this true?' Joseph said to her, 'Come and see.' The midwife went with him.

(19, 2) As they came to the cave, a bright cloud over-shadowed it, and the midwife said, 'Today my soul is magnified, because my eyes have seen marvels : salvation has come to Israel.' The cloud immediately disappeared, and its place was taken by a light so strong that their eyes could not bear it. Gradually the light went, and the child appeared, and it took the breast of its mother Mary. The midwife cried out, 'This is a great day : I have seen something entirely new.'

(19, 3) As the midwife came out of the cave, she met Salome and said to her, 'Salome, Salome, I have some-thing entirely new to tell you, something beyond the order of nature : a virgin has given birth.' Salome said, 'As God lives, unless I can test it with my finger, I will not believe that a virgin has given birth.'

(20, 1) So the midwife went in and told Mary, 'Get yourself ready because there is a great argument about you.' Salome went in and examined her with her finger, and cried out, 'What a wicked unbeliever I am! I have put the living God to the test, and look, my hand is dropping off as if it is on fire!' (20, 2) And she knelt down and prayed, 'God of my fathers, remember me. Do not shame me before your people but heal me. You know that it was in your name that I performed my task, and from you that I received my wages.' (20, 3)

An angel of the Lord stood before her and said, 'Salome, the Lord has heard your prayer. Come, touch the child with your hand and you will be healed.' (20, 4) She did so, and was healed as she had asked. As she left the cave, the angel cried out, 'Salome, Salome, tell no one the marvel you have seen until the child enters Jerusalem.'

(22, 3) When Elizabeth heard that John was being searched for (by Herod's soldiers), she took him and went up into the hill-country, looking about for a place to hide him. And finding none, she groaned aloud and said, 'Mountain of God, receive me, a mother, with my child.' The mountain immediately split open and received her, and a light shone upon them, for an angel of the Lord was there protecting them.

From *Serapion's Life of John* (Arabic translation of a Greek original of the fourth century).

After five years, Elizabeth died, and St John sat and wept since he did not know how to bury her, being only seven and a half years old. Herod also died the same day.

(From Egypt, the child Jesus), who can see heaven and earth, saw his cousin John weeping over his mother, and he also began to weep . . . His mother saw him and asked, 'Why are you weeping? Did the old man Joseph scold you, or someone else?' And the mouth that was full of life answered, 'No, mother, the real reason is that old Elizabeth your cousin has left my beloved John an orphan.'

On hearing this, the Virgin began to weep for her own cousin. Jesus said to her, 'Don't cry, my virgin mother, you will see her within the hour.' He was still speaking when a bright cloud came down . . . They mounted the cloud and flew to the desert of Ain Karim, where St

John was sitting by the body of blessed Elizabeth. The Saviour said to the cloud, 'Drop us this side of them.' It did so at once, and disappeared. But St John had heard the noise and had run off terrified. Then he heard a voice, 'Don't be afraid, John, it is Jesus Christ, your master. I am your cousin Jesus, and I have come to you with my beloved mother to attend to your mother's burial' . . . They washed the body of the blessed Elizabeth in the spring . . . The holy Virgin held John and wept over him, and cursed Herod for the numerous crimes he had committed.

Then Michael and Gabriel came down from heaven and dug a grave, and the Saviour said to them, 'Go and bring the souls of Zechariah and Simeon so that they can sing while you bury the body . . .' They shrouded the body of Elizabeth and sang . . .

Jesus Christ and his mother stayed with St John seven days and condoled with him over the death of his mother, and taught him how to live in the desert . . . Then they mounted the cloud . . . and it brought them to Nazareth.

From *The Martyrdom of Matthew* (possibly from the fifth century).

1. Jesus appeared to him (Matthew) in the form of one of the children that were singing in paradise . . . 3. Matthew said, 'I saw you in paradise singing with the other children that were killed in Bethlehem . . . Tell me, where is that ungodly Herod now?' 'He is in hell, in fire unquenchable, gehenna unending, boiling mud and the worm that never dies, because he killed 3000 children.'

From *The Gospel of Pseudo-Matthew* (original possibly fifth century Syriac).

(20, 1) On the third day of their journey (into Egypt), blessed Mary was worn out by the intense heat of the desert sun, and seeing a palm-tree she said to Joseph, 'Let me rest a little in the shade of this tree.' Joseph led her to the palm and she dismounted. When she had sat down, blessed Mary looked to the top of the palm, and seeing it thick with fruit said to Joseph, 'If only someone could fetch down some of that fruit.' Joseph replied, 'I am surprised you say that : look how high the tree is ! I am surprised you can even talk of fruit when all I can think of is water for ourselves and the animals : our water-bottles are almost dry.'

(20, 2) Then the child Jesus, sitting smiling in his mother's lap, said to the palm, 'Bend down your branches and refresh my mother with your fruit.' The palm obeyed his command at once, and bent down to Mary's feet. They all picked fruit and refreshed themselves. After they had finished the fruit, the tree remained bent, waiting for the command to return to its position. Then Jesus said, 'Rise up, stand upright, and join the other trees of mine in my Father's paradise. And open up the spring hidden in the earth beneath your roots, so that we can quench our thirst in its waters.' It arose at once, and a fountain of clear, fresh and sparkling water gushed out of its roots. They were glad at the sight, and all drank from it, the animals included, and gave thanks to God ...

(22, 1) As they journeyed on, Joseph said to Jesus, 'We are being roasted by this heat, my Lord. Do you agree that we should take the coast road? We may find some shelter in the towns there.' Jesus replied, 'Joseph, don't fear, I will shorten the route, and reduce into one day's journey what you thought would take thirty.' While they were speaking, they could already see the hills and cities of Egypt.

From *The Gospel of Thomas* (in a later Arabic translation).

One day when Jesus was running about and playing with some children, he passed by the workshop of a dyer called Salem, who had a number of lengths of cloth to be dyed. The Lord Jesus went into the dyer's workshop, took all the lengths, and put them into a vat of indigo. When Salem came and saw the cloth spoilt, he began to cry out, 'What have you done to me, son of Mary? . . .' The Lord Jesus replied, 'I will change the cloth into whatever colour you wish', and immediately began to take the lengths out of the vat, each of them dyed in the colour Salem had wanted.

One day the Lord Jesus went outdoors and saw some children who had gathered to play. He followed them, but they hid. The Lord Jesus came to the door of a house and saw some women standing there, and asked them where the children had gone. They said there was no one there . . . The Lord Jesus said, 'Come out to your shepherd, little goats.' The children came out in the form of goats and began to skip round him. The women . . . implored him saying, 'Lord Jesus, son of Mary, truly you are the Good Shepherd of Israel, but have mercy on your handmaids . . . and restore the children to their former state.' So the Lord Jesus said, 'Come, children, let's go and play.' And immediately, before the women's very eyes, the goats were changed back into children.

From *The Gospel of Thomas* (second or third century, original in Greek or Syriac).

(2, 1) When the boy Jesus was five years old, he was playing by a ford, and channelled the running water into a number of puddles, and made them clean by a single command.

(2, 2) He made some soft clay and fashioned twelve sparrows out of it. This was on a sabbath day. Many other children were playing with him. (2, 3) A Jew who saw him went off to tell his father Joseph . . . (2, 4) Joseph came and cried out, 'Why are you doing something that is forbidden on the sabbath?' But Jesus clapped his hands and cried out to the sparrows, 'Off with you!', and the sparrows flew off chirping. (2, 5) The Jews who saw this were amazed.

(3, 1) (A boy) took a willow-branch and scattered the water which Jesus had channelled into puddles. When Jesus saw this, he was infuriated and said, 'You insolent, godless fool, what harm did the water do you? Now you will wither like a willow-branch.'

(3, 3) Immediately the boy withered up, and Jesus returned home to Joseph. The parents of the boy, weeping over his young years, took him up and brought him to Joseph, saying, 'What sort of a child have you got, to do such things?'[3]

(4, 1) After this, as he was going through the village, a running child knocked against his shoulder. Jesus was enraged and said, 'That is as far as you will go', and the child immediately fell down and died. Those who saw this said, 'Where does this boy come from? Everything he says comes true.' (4, 2) The parents of the dead child came to Joseph saying, 'You cannot stay in the village with a boy like that, unless you teach him to bless instead of to curse. He is killing all our children.'

(5, 1) Joseph called the boy aside and reproached him, 'Why do you do things which hurt people and make

---

[3] In a later version, Jesus, not wishing to grieve his parents, kicks the boy on the back and bids him rise, which he does, while Jesus goes on playing with the water.

them hate and persecute us?' Jesus replied, 'They will get their punishment', and immediately his accusers were struck blind . . . (5, 2) Seeing this, Joseph took him by the ear and pulled hard. (5, 3) The child was infuriated and said . . . 'You know that I am not yours! Stop annoying me.'

(6, 1) A teacher called Zacchaeus said . . . (6, 2) 'Come, hand him over to me to teach him the alphabet and respect for his elders.' . . . (6, 3) Jesus looked at Zacchaeus and said, 'How can you, who do not even know the nature of Alpha, teach others Beta?' . . . (7, 2) Zacchaeus said, 'I thought I was getting a pupil : I find myself with a teacher . . . (7, 4) Take him home, Joseph. He is something out of the ordinary, a god, or an angel, or I don't know what.' (8, 1) The Jews tried to console Zacchaeus, but the child laughed out loud and said . . . 'I have come from above to curse them (the blind in heart) and call them to higher things.' . . . (8, 2) And immediately all those who had fallen under his curse were healed. After that no one dared provoke him, lest he should curse them and maim them.

(9, 1) Some days later Jesus was playing upstairs, and one of the children playing with him fell off the roof and died. The other children fled at the sight, and Jesus was left alone. (9, 2) The parents of the dead child came and accused him of throwing him down. Jesus denied it, but they continued to shout at him. (9, 3) So Jesus leapt down from the roof, and standing over the dead child cried out with a loud voice, 'Zeno (that was his name), get up and tell me, did I throw you down?' He got up at once and said, 'No, Lord, you did not throw me down, you raised me up.' . . .

(11, 1) When he was six years old, his mother gave him a pitcher to bring home water. (11, 2) But in the crowd he stumbled and broke the pitcher. So Jesus spread out the cloak he was wearing, put the water in it, and brought it to his mother. His mother, seeing the miracle, kissed him, and treasured the mystery in her heart.

(12, 1) In the spring the child went out with his father to sow wheat in their field. As his father sowed, the child Jesus sowed one grain of wheat. (12, 2) When he had reaped and threshed it, he brought in a hundred measures. He called in all the poor of the village and gave them wheat, and Joseph kept the rest. He was eight years old when he worked this miracle.

(13, 1) His father was a carpenter, and at that time made ploughs and yokes. A rich man commissioned him to make him a bed. Joseph cut one beam shorter than the other and did not know what to do. The child Jesus said to his father, 'Put the two pieces on the ground and even them off at your end.' (13, 2) Joseph did as the child told him. Jesus stood at the other end, took hold of the shorter piece, and stretched it until it was the same length as the other. His father Joseph was amazed at the sight. He embraced the child and kissed him, saying, 'How happy I am that God has given me this child' . . .

(14, 2) Jesus said to (another teacher), 'If you are a real teacher, and if you know the alphabet well, tell me what Alpha means and I will tell you what Beta means.' The teacher was annoyed and hit him on the head. The child was hurt, and cursed him, and he immediately collapsed and fell to the ground. (14, 3) The child returned home to Joseph, who was grieved and told his mother, 'Don't let him go outdoors. Everyone who annoys him dies.'

(15, 1) Another teacher, a good friend of Joseph, said, 'Bring the child to my school, perhaps I shall succeed in teaching him his letters.' Joseph told him, 'Brother, if you are not afraid, take him.' He took him gingerly. (15, 2) The child went gladly and boldly into the school, and found a book on the reading-desk. He took it up, but instead of reading the text began to speak in the power of the Holy Spirit and to teach the Law to the by-standers. A large crowd assembled and stood listening, amazed at the fluency and the grace of his teaching, coming as it did from a mere child. (15, 3) When Joseph heard of it, he ran to the school, fearing that this teacher too would be maimed. But the teacher said to Joseph, 'Brother, I took in this child as a pupil, but he is full of grace and wisdom. I beg you, take him home.' (15, 4) When the child heard this, he smiled at him and said, 'You have spoken the truth, and so for your sake the one that was struck will also be healed.' And immediately the other teacher was healed . . .

(17, 1) A little child was sick and died . . . Jesus touched his breast and said, 'Don't die, but live and be with your mother.' It looked up at once and laughed. He said to the woman, 'Take him and give him some milk, and re-member me' . . . (17, 2) And Jesus went off to play with the other children.

(18, 1) A house was being built, and there was a disaster. Jesus got up and went there, and saw a man lying dead. He said, 'Young man, I'm telling you to get up. Back to work.' He got up at once and worshipped him. (18, 2) The crowd who saw this were amazed and said, 'This child is from heaven. He has saved many souls from death, and will continue to do so as long as he lives.'

(19, 1) When he was twelve years old, his parents went according to custom to Jerusalem . . . (etc. as in Luke 2 :42ff)

From *Pistis Sophia* (a Gnostic work of the third century). 61. Mary said to Jesus : When you were small, before the Spirit had come upon you, while you were with Joseph

in the vineyard, the Spirit came from heaven into my
house. He looked just like you, so that I did not recognize him, thinking he was you. The Spirit said to me,
'Where is my brother Jesus? I want to meet him.' When
he said this, I was puzzled, and thought a ghost had
come to tempt me. So I seized him and tied him to the
foot of the bed at home, and went out to you and Joseph,
and found you in the vineyard where Joseph was putting up a fence. When you heard me speak to Joseph,
you knew what it was about, and with great joy you said,
'Where is he? I want to see him. I was expecting him
here.' When Joseph heard you say this, he was puzzled,
and we went up together to the house, where we found
the Spirit still tied to the bed. We looked at you and
at him, and found you were just like him. When we
freed him from the bed, he embraced you and kissed
you, and you kissed him, and you both became one.

From a *Sermon of Cyril of Alexandria* (fifth century, in
Coptic).
Mary used to take hold of his hand and lead him along
the roads, saying, 'My sweet son, walk a little', just as all
other babies are taught to walk. And he, Jesus, God
himself, happily followed her. He clung to her with his
little fingers, stopping from time to time, and hanging
on to the skirts of his mother Mary, he on whom the
whole universe depends. He would look up into her face
. . . and she would catch him up to her breast, and walk
along with him in her arms.

6. Where Have All the Angels Gone?

In a 1969 Peanuts cartoon, Linus is speaking to Charlie Brown's sister Sally who has just begun kindergarten: 'You don't *believe* in the story of the Great Pumpkin? . . . I'm disillusioned! I thought little girls always believed everything that was told to them . . . I thought little girls were innocent and trusting . . .' Sally's reply comes in the last frame: 'Welcome to 1969.' If educators today are having problems with certain theological questions, it is not because they have dreamed them up out of the blue. The very people they are teaching, even the children of 1969 let alone those of later decades, are pushing them to ask these questions.

WHAT ABOUT THE ANGELS?

In a treatise such as this on the Christmas stories, busy as they are with the flurry of angels' wings, it is appropriate that the topic should be dealt with at some length. I call it appropriate because I seem to have spent my life – and other theologians have no doubt had the same experience – fending off the question of angels at the most inappropriate moments. Whether I have been lecturing on Job, or the Psalms, or the shape of Mark's gospel, or the journeys of St Paul, or the Trinity, or whatever, someone could be relied upon in question time to ask, 'What about the angels?', in something of the same way as any political meeting could be relied upon to produce, eventually, the question, 'What about the workers?'

At the beginning I regarded it as a kind of maverick or rogue question, which might just as easily have been, 'What about the tower of Babel?' or 'What about Mary Magdalene?' as if the answer could make all that difference. But the strange persistence of the question forced me to see that it had a deeper significance, that what the questioners were asking me again and again was, 'What about the supernatural?' If what was being said on Job (or the Psalms or Mark or Paul or the Trinity or whatever) was more and more secular, less and less supernatural, then the question could be a sort of touchstone. To admit that, after all, the angels still kept their accustomed places would at least safeguard the supernatural and guarantee that God continues to intervene. To deny that would really be the end. What about the angels?

ANGELS GALORE

The four chapters devoted to the Christmas stories in Matthew and Luke contain more references to angels than any other page in the four gospels. Luke mentions angels fourteen times : four times the angel Gabriel's annunciation to Zechariah, five times the angel Gabriel's annunciation to Mary, and five times the angel's annunciation to the shepherds. Matthew mentions them four times, twice the angel encouraging Joseph to marry Mary, once the angel warning Joseph to escape to Egypt, and once the angel telling him that the situation allowed him to return.

What is interesting is that the only other pages of the gospel which can remotely compare with these opening pages for their profusion of angels are the closing pages, with their account of the resurrection. There Matthew mentions them twice, Luke once and John once. If we added the 'young man' at the tomb in Mark and the 'two men in white' in Luke's account of the ascension, it would make seven appearances in all.

What is most interesting of all is that in the rest of the gospel narrative angels scarcely get a look in. They are occasionally referred to ('The Son of Man will come with the angels', 'There will be joy before the angels', etc.), but they have no walking-on part. The only exceptions are the comforting angels in Matthew's account of the Temptation (4 : 11) and in Luke's account of the Agony (22 : 43 – though even here some ancient manuscripts omit this verse).

It might be enlightening to ask ourselves why these two events to which there were explicitly no witnesses (the Temptation and the Agony), and why those two stories which in the nature of things could not be recorded in the ordinary sense of the word (the birth of the messiah and his resurrection) should be expressed in terms of angels. Perhaps we can find the answer to this question by examining, at least in outline, the history of angelology. Before we can answer, 'Where have all the angels gone?' we must ask, 'Where did all the angels come from?'

WHEN THERE WERE NO ANGELS

Once upon a time, there were no angels. At least not in the story. The story of Israel was able to be told simply in terms of God and man, without the intervention of any angels, until very late in their history. The word 'angel' does not occur in the preaching of any of the prophets until the time of the Babylonian exile about

600 B.C., that is to say three quarters of the way through Israel's biblical history.

How angels first began to appear in the story is best understood by looking at a number of texts. There are texts which, in one telling of the event, give the walking-on part to God, and in the other to the angel, while God stays in the wings. For instance, the story of the conflict between Sarah and Hagar, which is at one time told in these terms:

'Drive away that slave-girl (Hagar) and her son (Ishmael),' (Sarah) said to Abraham; 'This slave-girl's son is not to share the inheritance with my son Isaac.' This greatly distressed Abraham because of his son, but *God* said to him, 'Do not distress yourself . . . the slave-girl's son I will also make into a nation, for he is your child too' . . . Abraham took some bread and a skin of water and, giving them to Hagar, he put the child on her shoulder and sent her away. She wandered off into the wilderness of Beersheba. When the skin of water was finished she abandoned the child under a bush . . . saying . . . 'I cannot see the child die'. So she sat at a distance; and the child wailed and wept. But *God* heard the boy wailing, and . . . called to Hagar from heaven . . . 'Do not be afraid, for *God* has heard (Yishma-el) the boy's cry . . . I will make him into a great nation.' Then *God* opened Hagar's eyes and she saw a well, so she went and filled the skin with water and gave the boy a drink (Genesis 21 : 10-19)

appears in another chapter in the following terms:

Sarai said to Abram, '. . . I count for nothing in her eyes' . . . 'Very well,' Abram said to Sarai, 'your slave-

girl is at your disposal. Treat her as you think fit.'
Sarai accordingly treated her so badly that she ran
away from her. *The angel of the Lord* met her near
a spring in the wilderness . . . He said, 'Hagar . . .
where are you going?' 'I am running away from my
mistress Sarai' she replied. *The angel of the Lord*
said to her, 'Go back to your mistress and submit to
her.' *The angel of the Lord* said to her, 'I will make
your descendants too numerous to be counted.' Then
the angel of the Lord said to her . . . 'You will bear
a son and you shall name him Ishmael, for the Lord
has heard your cries of distress.' . . . The well is . . .
between Kadesh and Bered. (Genesis 16 :5-14)

Again, the famous episode under the oak tree at Mamre,
which is here described in terms of the Lord :

The Lord appeared to (Abraham) at the Oak of
Mamre . . . 'My lord,' (Abraham) said 'I beg you, if I
find favour with you, kindly do not pass your servant
by. A little water shall be brought; you shall wash
your feet and lie down under the tree.' . . . Then his
guest said, 'I shall visit you again next year without
fail, and your wife will then have a son.' . . . *The Lord*
asked Abraham, 'Why did Sarah laugh? . . . Is anything too wonderful for *the Lord*?' . . . Then *the Lord*
said, 'How great an outcry there is against Sodom . . .'
(Genesis 18 :1, 3, 10-14, 20)

is the same story as that told in the following terms,
though as the text now stands the two stories have been
interwoven :

(Abraham) looked up, and there he saw *three men*
standing near him. As soon as he saw them he ran

from the entrance of the tent to meet them, and
bowed to the ground . . . Then taking cream, milk and
the calf he had prepared, he laid all before them, and
they ate . . . 'Where is your wife Sarah?' they asked
him. 'She is in the tent', he replied . . . From there
the men set out and arrived within sight of Sodom,
with Abraham accompanying them to show them the
way . . . The angels reached Sodom . . . (Genesis
18 :2, 8-9, 16, 19 :1)

Again, the last of the plagues of Egypt, which in one
version is attributed to the Lord :

The Lord said to Moses . . . 'That night, I will go
through the land of Egypt and strike down all the
first-born in the land of Egypt, man and beast alike,
and I shall deal out punishment to all the gods of
Egypt, I am *the Lord* . . . You shall escape the
destroying plague when I strike the land of Egypt'
(Exodus 12 :12-13)

is in other versions attributed to ministerial angels :

(The Lord) will . . . not allow *the Destroyer* to enter
your homes and strike (Exodus 12 :23)

He let loose on them (the Egyptians) . . . a company of
destroying angels . . . (and) gave their lives over to
the plague (Psalm 78 :49).

Those, then, are examples of different versions of the
same story disagreeing about whether the action is to be
attributed to God or to the angel. But there are even
more interesting examples of one and the same version
of a story making no distinction at all between God and

the angel, and using the words 'God' and 'angel' as if
they were completely interchangeable. For example, one
of the stories of Hagar quoted above is told consistently
in terms of 'the angel of the Lord' ('The angel of the
Lord met her . . . The angel of the Lord said to her . . .
Then the angel of the Lord said to her . . .'). Yet it con-
cludes:

> Hagar gave a name to *the Lord* who had spoken to
> her, 'You are El Roi . . . the *God* who sees me.'
> (Genesis 16:13)

Similarly, in the story of the sacrifice of Isaac, although
it is the angel of the Lord who speaks throughout, it is
the very voice of God that is heard:

> The angel of the Lord called to him from heaven . . .
> 'Now I know you fear God. You have not refused *me*
> . . . your only son.' . . . Abraham called this place '*The
> Lord* provides' . . . The angel of the Lord called
> Abraham a second time from heaven. 'I swear by my
> *own self* – it is *the Lord* who speaks – because you
> have . . . not refused *me* your only son . . .' (Genesis
> 22:11-16)

Again, in the story of the vocation of Moses, it is the
angel of the Lord who appears, but it is the Lord himself
who sees him and speaks to him:

> The angel of the Lord appeared to him in the shape of
> a flame of fire coming from the middle of a bush . . .
> 'I must go and look at this strange sight,' Moses said
> . . . Now *the Lord* saw him go forward to look, and
> called to him from the middle of the bush. 'Moses,
> Moses!' (Exodus 3:2-5)

Once more, in the story of the annunciation of the birth
of Samson which has already been quoted above in the
discussion of Luke's annunciation story, the entire narrative is again told in terms of 'the angel of the Lord'.
('The angel of the Lord appeared . . . His presence was
like the presence of the angel of God . . . The angel of
the Lord visited the woman again . . . Manoah then said
to the angel of the Lord . . . Manoah did not know this
was the angel of the Lord . . . The angel of the Lord
ascended in the flame.') Yet the climax of the story is
expressed in the words:

> Manoah and his wife fell face downwards on the
> ground . . . and Manoah said . . . 'We are certain to
> die, because we have seen *God*.' (Judges 13:21-2)

Reference to a concordance under the word 'angel' will
reveal many other examples of this phenomenon.

What has happened here? Given the fact that in
almost all the cases quoted it has been a question not of
an angel but of *the* angel – there is only the one – he
would seem to be a sort of double for God, an *alter ego*,
an extension of God, indistinguishable from the God he
represents. Why has he been brought in? Is it out of
respect, in order to safeguard the transcendence of God
which would be endangered if God himself was brought
too close to men? Or is it out of a need for the visual, to
give expression to the intervention of a God who is by
definition invisible? Or is it out of a loss of nerve, out of
a feeling that so much power concentrated in one point
was too dangerous, and needed to be filtered, diluted and
mediated if man was to make safe contact with it?

Whichever it was, the word 'angel' clearly corresponds
to a human need, the need to make God intelligible. All
the texts quoted above are about God, not about some-

one else. Yet the existence, nature and activity of this
God, mystery that he is, must be expressed in human
terms. What other terms have we got?

BABYLONIANS AND PERSIANS

In the telling of the story of Israel, then, angels seem to
have arisen out of the need to speak in human language
of the reality of God. Further developments in angelology were made possible during the period in which
Israel came into contact with Babylonia and Persia, from
the sixth century B.C. onwards.

The Babylonian influence will be recognized by anyone familiar with the gigantic and forbidding sphinx-
like stone creatures, with a human head, a lion's body, a
bull's feet and an eagle's wings, which have been brought
to many of our western museums from Babylonia. There
they used to guard the doorways of royal palaces, and
were known as *Karibu*. The word was transliterated into
Hebrew as *Cherubim* or *Seraphim* (both words would
seem to have the same derivation – it is probable that the
mythological word *griffin* has the same origin) and as
such eventually made its way into angel-language. But in
its origin the word and what it stood for was simply a
striking symbol which spelled out the message 'Royal En-
closure'. As such it provided an apt imagery to express
the majesty of God, and it is used in this sense in the
Eden story where the *cherubim* forbid entrance to the
presence of God (Genesis 3 :24), in the desert story where
two gold *cherubim* mark the presence of God in the Ark
of the Covenant (Exodus 25 :18), and in the temple story
where God both enters on the *cherubim* (1 Kings 8 :7ff),
and later uses them as his means of leaving there in order
to settle among the community of the exiles (Ezekiel

10-11). The *Cherubim* and the *Seraphim* are a borrowed imagery to express the presence, power and activity of God.

Persian art is less well represented in our museums, but its influence on Old Testament angelology was dramatic, for it was responsible for introducing wings. Until then, angels had to make do with ladders or stairways to come from heaven and return there. Jacob's dream in Genesis 28 : 12 illustrates this well.

Persian religion had a whole host of spirits and genies, majestic winged creatures that formed a kind of heavenly retinue and an army of intermediaries between heaven and earth. It was in imitation of them that the angels of Israel not only grew wings but multiplied into a vast celestial court, numbering thousands upon thousands and myriads upon myriads. The unapproachable majesty of God was certainly enhanced thereby.

But this development left the angels rather impersonal, and in compensation a number of names begin to emerge at this time to take the place previously occupied by the one 'angel of the Lord': Michael the symbol of God's judgement and protection of Israel (Daniel 10 : 13), Gabriel the symbol of God's self-communication (Daniel 8 : 15, 9 : 21), and Raphael the symbol of God's healing and companionship (Tobit 3 : 25).

Those for whom the word 'angel' evokes images usually connected with Christmas decorations would do well to remember that at this stage of the history of angelology we still remain in the realm of awe, majesty and magnificence. The word 'angel' was not meant to make people gush, but blench. The feeling is well conveyed in these lines written in this period of Israelite history :

I raised my eyes to look about me, and this is what I saw : A man dressed in linen, with a girdle of pure gold round his waist; his body was like beryl, his face shone like lightning his eyes were like fiery torches, his arms and his legs had the gleam of burnished bronze, the sound of his voice was like the noise of a crowd. I, Daniel, alone saw the apparition; the men who were with me did not see the apparition, but so great a trembling overtook them that they fled to hide. I was left alone, gazing on this great apparition; I was powerless, my appearance altered out of all recognition, what strength I had deserted me. I heard him speak, and at the sound of his voice I fell unconscious to the ground. (Daniel 10 :5-9)

ANGELS IN THE NEW TESTAMENT

It is this language of the later writings of the Old Testament that is picked up by the writers of the New. The word 'angel' means for them what it meant for the post-exile prophets : the majesty and transcendence of God, the communication and revelation of God, the protection and care of God. In the gospel pages, as has been pointed out, angel-language is concentrated most on the narratives of the nativity and the resurrection, where the world of God and the world of men are brought closest together. Outside of the gospels angels abound most in the pages of the book of Revelation, which is explicitly a book of poetry and visions.

But it is St Paul who contributed most to the future development of angelology by introducing to us the names of Thrones, Dominations, Principalities, Powers and Virtues (Ephesians 1 :21, Colossians 1 :16). Not that he puts these forward for our veneration. On the contrary, these for him were the rival attractions which the Gnostic heretics of his time were offering for worship, and which he insists have no more validity or future once God has revealed himself in Christ. But the names were all to provide grist for the mill of future angelologists.

ANGELS IN THE MIDDLE AGES

Angels enjoyed their greatest vogue in the Middle Ages. One writer has expressed it colourfully by pointing out that the English farmer of 1300 believed more firmly that there were angels in Kent than that there were other farmers in France and Italy.

It was a time when the vast amount of accumulated knowledge, speculation and what was assumed to be revealed information on the subject was reduced into some kind of order, and the nine choirs of angels were established. This was done very simply by counting up the titles to be found in the pages of the Bible and giving them a hierarchical order, with the Seraphim and Cherubim at the top, St Paul's Thrones, Dominations, Virtues, Powers and Principalities in the middle, and ordinary Archangels and Angels at the bottom, making nine in all. Very conveniently, since the universe had also been analysed and found to be made up of nine concentric spheres, it gave each choir a sphere to be responsible for.

It was the time when their number was specified : indeed, since they were non-reproductive, this number had to have been fixed from the moment of creation. The Bible had spoken of legions of angels, each comprising a myriad (ten thousand) angels. Since each of the nine choirs was computed as consisting of a myriad legions, this made a population of 900 million angels in all, just falling short of the present combined population of the Commonwealth and the E.E.C., with the shortfall likely to increase. Of these, 300 million were deduced to be fallen angels from the description in Revelation 12 :4 : 'His (Satan's) tail dragged a third of the stars from the sky.'

It was a time when their nature was closely analysed. In an exhaustive treatise of seventy-two articles, admittedly an excuse for asking some deeply philosophical questions about time, place, movement and above all knowledge, St Thomas Aquinas delves into such fascinating problems as whether angels are partly bodily (no) or pure spirit (yes), whether they can assume bodies (yes) and whether these are living bodies (no), whether angels can be in several places at once (no) and whether several angels can be in the same place at once (no), whether they can move from place to place (yes) and whether this is instantaneous (no), how exactly they know God themselves and things other than themselves, whether they know the future and the secrets of men's hearts (no) and whether they can be mistaken (no), whether they have free will (yes) and whether they can get angry (no), whether they were created in grace (yes) and whether they can sin (yes), what sort of sin they committed and whether more sinned than remained in grace (no).

It was a time when tasks were assigned to the various choirs, and this magnificent protocol was drawn up for Michael : 'Chief of the Archangels, Head of the Order of Virtues, Captain of the Heavenly Host, Holy Standard-Bearer, Prince of the Presence, Conqueror of Lucifer, Safeguard against the Wickedness and Snares of the Devil, Angel of Repentance, Righteousness, Mercy and Sanctification.' There is a sense of anticlimax in the addition made to these credentials by Pope Pius XII in 1950 : 'patron of policemen.'

ANGELS IN THE RENAISSANCE

This unprecedented prestige of the angels suffered a sharp decline during the Renaissance, when men's eyes began to turn from heaven and focus on the earth. The art of the period indicates the extent to which the angels were gradually humanized. It was the age of the rediscovery of the art of Greek and Roman antiquity, and the austere and hieratic figures of the past slowly began to take on the shape and characteristics of the Roman cupids, the winged symbols of innocence and love.

Under this influence it was difficult to make an angel look as if he belonged in heaven any more. The annual rash of feathered dolls with which we today mark our Christmas, both commercially and devotionally, is only the long-term result of this decline. What was once a word which filled people with awe now only makes their eyes mist over. Angels have become winged babies, smothered in a welter of tinsel, designed mainly to keep the children happy.

ANGELS AND THE REFORMERS

The Reformation was a reaction against many undesirable developments in medieval doctrine and practice, not least that of angelology. Luther's insistence that men have direct access to God by faith, that they do not need mediators upon mediators, that 'neither death, nor life, nor angels, nor principalities, nor powers . . . shall be able to separate us from the love of God' (Romans 8 : 38), because these are simply servants of God whereas man is a *son* of God, tied by blood to Christ Jesus – this was a shattering insight into the centrality of Christ. But it left the angels theologically unemployed. Whatever their role or meaning had been, it had been taken over by Christ. Are we only today reaping the fruits of this insight?

ANGEL-LANGUAGE

After this rapid survey of the history of angelology, perhaps some provisional conclusions may be made. The history has indicated how the term 'angel' originated and developed. Angels were 'born' out of the human need to speak of God in human language, the language of poetry and symbolism, which is able to visualize the Invisible, to exteriorize the Inner Voice, to personify the Mystery that lies at the heart of all things.

In essence, therefore, angels are a language about God, not about themselves. The most prominent name in the mythology of angels emphasizes this: the word Michael means literally, 'Who is like God?', in other words, 'Nothing takes the place of God, not even me.'

Of God the language of angels says this: that he is a reality to be adored and praised; that he transcends all that is human with a majesty beyond that of all earthly kings and rulers; that he is nonetheless present among men not distant from them, knowing them and revealing himself to them not hiding from them; that his power and activity are exercised here on earth not in heaven; that his power is to protect and support and lead men to union with himself.

The task of an angel is not to keep God at a safe distance, but to bring him to men. To read something about angels is to read something about God.

This identification of the angels with God is characteristic of the Bible. It is significant that the further one goes from the Bible the less true this becomes : in patristic and medieval and scholastic theology angels tend more and more to come between God and men, to take on an entity of their own and so to remove God from the world. It is significant that for those writers who have remained close to the Bible the angels have remained a symbolic language speaking of the presence and self-communication of God. The Talmudic sayings : 'Every blade of grass has its angel that bends over it and whispers, "Grow, grow" ', 'A new angel is born with every word that God speaks', contrast strongly with the scholastic speculations about when and how and at what limit the number of the angels was fixed.

ANGELS OUTSIDE THE STORY

I have referred to the angels as a symbolic language, the language of poetry. But we must go further and ask whether anything objective corresponds to this poetic language. In other words, we have so far considered angels and their meaning inside the story only. But what do they do and mean outside the story? Do they exist at all outside the story?

Some may feel that we are not free to ask that question, that the question is out of order because the existence of angels has been defined by Church authority. But clearly any Church document which has something to say about angels must be interpreted in terms of the knowledge and ideas of the time in which it was drafted. No Church document or definition can speak in a timeless manner, outside of its own context. And if a doctrinal definition simply repeats the language of the Bible, it presumably has no further information to offer, and adds nothing to what an analysis of the Bible can reveal.

In actual fact, the documents of the Catholic Church that have something to say about angels are very restrained in their language and speak in very generalized terms. The reference to angels occurs only four times, in texts which deal with the doctrine of creation. The Fourth Lateran Council in 1215 defined the Christian faith as belief in a God who is the creator of all things, visible and invisible, bodily and spiritual, worldly and angelic. This wording was simply taken up and repeated, without further specification, in the Councils of Florence in 1440, of Trent in 1564, and of First Vatican in 1870.

Anyone who wishes to take these definitions seriously will want to know to what these statements of his forefathers bind him. Some think that they bind the believer to the existence of an objective world of spirits, good and evil, who influence our world and all its history from their own invisible world, and who objectively enter into our world from time to time to execute God's will.

Others are convinced that there is no need to take the documents so literally, that like scripture they speak in symbolic language, and that the believer is therefore free either to leave the question of the objective existence of angels entirely open (they may or may not exist, who knows?), or even to deny it altogether as inconsistent with his understanding of himself and his world, and with the way in which God has revealed himself as acting in this world.

ARE ANGELS OUT?

Anyone who takes this radical view, that angels are

'only' a language, might be tempted to conclude that all the stories about angels have become redundant and should be scrapped. This would indeed be drastic. He would get rid not only of the angels but of the very ideas that they stand for. And since those ideas are about God, he would be in danger of getting rid of God. For angels stand for the belief that there are in our lives forces beyond our apprehension,

> that there's always an inside to events, a personal as well as an impersonal aspect, a spiritual as well as a material, that the entire universe is shot through with God and his living activity . . . (Angels are) a biblical way of denying a final materialism, the belief that everything can be explained by the outside of events, merely in terms of the physical and the impersonal. (*But That I Can't Believe* by J. A. T. Robinson, pp. 93 and 94)

How can such a conviction be expressed in concrete or visual terms except by speaking of something like an angel? If only the language of poetry and symbolism can preserve for people the conviction that there are dimensions in our lives beyond those which can be measured or expressed in scientific terms, are they not right to insist on keeping the angels intact in paintings and mosaics, in liturgy and the roofs of churches, and above all in the Bible stories? It would be a ham-handed literalist who would want to do away with them.

As long as we remain aware that the angels do stand for this conviction, and never for themselves. Angels never speak about themselves, only about God. We do not know what angels are, only what they mean: the majesty and the transcendence, the protection and the revelation of God. And the stories ensure that this truth can not only be expressed but preserved as they are handed on from one generation to the next.

The stories can, of course, be ruined by trying to rationalize them, by trying to take them quite literally but explaining everything in them in such a sweetly reasonable way that all the mystery goes out of them. So the young man sitting at the open tomb of Jesus is no longer an angel but a white-shirted passer-by. Similarly the annunciation is no longer a message from heaven but an early example of extra-sensory perception. And the shepherds' vision in the fields is not of a choir of angels but of an unidentified flying object.

This is indeed, and with a vengeance, the estranged face missing 'the many-splendoured thing'! The magic has gone. Life has been reduced to its prosaic three dimensions, and miserably impoverished. To eliminate the mystery is to eliminate God. Because the activity of God cannot be expressed in terms which would rationalize everything, only in poetry and symbols. To find out the meaning of Shelley's description of a skylark, 'bird thou never wert', one would not go to an ornithologist.

It is that hidden divine reality that the New Testament authors are trying to evoke when they use angel-language to speak of the birth of Jesus.

7. The Story of Jesus' Virgin Birth

In telling their Christmas stories, both Matthew and Luke speak of Jesus being conceived by and born of a virgin. Matthew tells the story in these words:

> This is how Jesus Christ came to be born. His mother Mary was betrothed to Joseph; but *before* they came to live together she was found to be with child *through the Holy Spirit* . . . 'Do not be afraid to take Mary home as your wife, because she has conceived what is in her *by the Holy Spirit*' . . . this took place to fulfil the words spoken by the Lord through the prophet: *The virgin* will conceive and give birth to a son . . . and though he had *not had intercourse* with her, she gave birth to a son. (Matthew 1:18, 20-5)

Luke's story is as follows:

> A *virgin* betrothed to a man named Joseph . . . and the *virgin's* name was Mary . . . 'Mary . . . you are to conceive and bear a son' . . . 'How can this come about, since I am a *virgin*?' 'The *Holy Spirit* will come upon you . . . and so the child will be . . . called *Son of God* . . . nothing is impossible to God' . . . Jesus was about thirty years old, being the son, *as it was thought*, of Joseph (whose genealogy follows). (Luke 1:27, 34-8, 3:23)

Since the subject is a complex one, and is receiving considerable attention from theologians at the moment, I thought it would be desirable to devote a separate chapter to a discussion of the question.

GETTING THE SUBJECT STARTED

Perhaps the discussion could best begin by stating that it is extremely difficult to begin! Many people, particularly Catholics, put up such psychological barriers at this point that it makes it more than usually difficult to get the subject started.

I remember the time when I was in charge of building a church for a small country parish, and my parishioners and I were faced with the problem of providing a fitting representation of Christ for the reredos of the sanctuary, and of our Lady for a statue to be placed in the aisle. The Christ gave us no difficulty whatever. The artist who worked for us gave us a rather unusual painting, majestic, strong and deliberately un-pretty. A bearded Russián in the village had posed as a model. After an initial moment of surprise, it was very easily accepted. But we had enormous trouble over the Madonna, because everyone knew that in this case certain things simply would not be acceptable, that you could go wrong far more easily on our Lady than on Christ. People feel here an emotional involvement which makes them far more ready to take offence, and far less open to discussion.

A beautiful piece of Brendan Behan's writing (*Borstal Boy*, Hutchinson, London, 1958, pp. 58-9) illustrates the same point. As an I.R.A. man caught in England during the troubles of the late 1930s, he is in Walton gaol awaiting trial. Being a Catholic by upbringing, he is able to describe the Sunday Mass he is about to attend with a serene buoyancy. But no sooner does he mention our Lady (and indeed it would seem that for him Mass is simply identified with praying to our Lady) than he is away into an ecstatic rhapsody from which it would be extremely difficult to recall him by rational argument :

Mooney the screw stood in the hall, and shouted, 'R.C.s fall in for morning service, bring your prayer books and your 'ymn books.' I had not seen the priest yet, so I had no prayer book or hymn book.

But I did not want any prayer book to follow the Mass. That was the same the whole world over, from one end of it to another.

I had been extra religious when a kid, and the day I made my First Communion I had prayed to God to take me, as Napoleon prayed, when I would go straight to Heaven. I was a weekly communicant for years after, and in spasms, especially during Lent, a daily one . . . I had never given up the Faith (for what would I give it up for?) and now I was glad that even in this well-washed smelly English hell-hole of old Victorian cruelty, I had the Faith to fall back on. Every Sunday and holiday, I would be at one with hundreds of millions of Catholics, at the sacrifice of the Mass, to worship the God of our ancestors, and to pray to our Lady, the delight of the Gael, the consolation of mankind, the mother of God and of man, the pride of poets and artists, Dante, Villon, Eoghan Ruadh O Sullivan, in warmer, more humorous parts of the world than this nineteenth century English lavatory, in Florence, in France, in Kerry, where the arbutus grows and the fuchsia glows on the dusty hedges in the soft light of the summer evening.

It is that emotional problem which faces us as we

approach the question of the virgin birth. Some people feel that it is not a question which ought to be discussed. The matter is not open for analysis. It would be trespassing on sacred ground. Indeed the suggestion will make many people react in the same way as they would to having their own mother discussed in public. Christ yes, the resurrection yes, the Trinity yes. But not the Blessed Virgin Mary. The reaction is mentioned here so that the reader may sympathize with it, even if he does not share it.

Linked to this psychological problem is the further problem of putting the question the right way round. The subject of the virgin birth is difficult to get started not only because people feel personally involved, but because the question is often wrongly put. 'Do you believe in the virgin birth?' is for many Christians one of those questions expecting the answer yes, the word 'yes' meaning for them an unqualified acceptance of the virgin birth as they understand it. For such people, anyone who hesitates is lost and consigned to the outer darkness with other heretics. Because to wish to qualify that yes is regarded as a no.

Yet the fact is that the virgin birth, like so many other Christian doctrines, is not a 'yes or no' question. For a Christian can be utterly committed to what the doctrine is about, and yet realize that very often the traditional way of stating it has put the crunch at the wrong place.

This chapter is concerned with trying to put the crunch at the right place, with trying to ask the question in such a way that a more worthwhile answer can be given. I can only hope that no reader will take offence at this. None is intended. I wish to approach the question as reverently as I would my own mother.

'MIRACULOUS' BIRTHS

It was suggested above that the New Testament Christmas stories cannot be properly understood unless they are set against the background of the Old Testament, on which they are a meditation. This is particularly true of the virgin birth story, which does not exist in the abstract but is told in the context of a whole series of God-given births, births which are said to come about through the intervention of God.

Some of these have already been referred to above. The others should be set down here so that the background is complete. Of Cain's birth, for instance, it is said that 'The man had intercourse with his wife Eve, and she conceived and gave birth to Cain ('Acquisition'), saying, "I have acquired a man with the help of the Lord."' (Genesis 4:1) The phrase is the same as that which is used in the more familiar 'conceived by the Holy Spirit'. The birth of his brother Seth is spoken of in similar terms : 'Adam had intercourse with his wife, and she gave birth to a son whom she named Seth ('Gift'), saying, "*God* (not Adam) has granted me other offspring in place of Abel."' (Genesis 4:25)

The birth stories of the patriarchs Isaac, Jacob and Joseph have the same emphasis : 'Abraham and Sarah were old . . . past the age of child-bearing . . . The Lord asked, "Is anything too wonderful for the Lord? . . . Sarah will have a son."' And when the boy Isaac ('Joy') is born, Sarah says, '*God* (not Abraham) has given me cause to laugh.' (Genesis 18:11-14, 21:6) Later, Isaac's wife Rebekah is barren and 'Isaac prayed to the Lord on behalf of his wife . . . *The Lord* heard his prayer, and his wife Rebekah conceived . . . and they named him

Jacob.' (Genesis 25 :21-6) Later, Jacob fathers ten sons, but none by his favourite wife Rachel, who remains barren. 'Then *God* remembered Rachel; he heard her and opened her womb. She conceived and gave birth to a son . . . she named him Joseph ('Another'), saying, "May *God* (not Jacob) give me another"', which he eventually does (Genesis 30 :22-4).

Samson's birth is told in similar terms : '(Manoah's) wife was barren, she had borne no children. The angel of the Lord appeared to (her) and said . . . "You will conceive and bear a son . . . It is he who will begin to save Israel" . . . Manoah said to his wife . . . "we have seen *God*."' (Judges 13 :2-5, 22) So also is the birth of Samuel, whose mother Hannah 'the Lord had made . . . barren . . . She prayed to the Lord with many tears . . . Eli . . . said, ". . . May the *God* of Israel grant what you have asked of him" . . . and the Lord was mindful of her. She conceived and gave birth to a son, and called him Samuel ('Heard of God') "since", she said, "I asked the Lord for him" . . . Then Hannah said this prayer, "My heart exults in the Lord . . . *The Lord* gives death and life."' (1 Samuel 1 :5-20, 2 :1-6)

Towards the end of the Old Testament story, the mother of the Maccabee martyrs speaks of the birth of her children in these terms : 'I do not know how you appeared in my womb; it was not I who endowed you with breath and life . . . It is the *creator* of the world, ordaining the process of man's birth.' (2 Maccabees 7 : 22-3) Similarly John the Baptist's story begins, as we have seen, in these terms : '(Zechariah and Elizabeth) were childless : Elizabeth was barren and they were both getting on in years . . . The angel of the Lord said . . . "Zechariah . . . Your prayer has been heard. Your wife Elizabeth is to bear you a son and you must name him John ('Yahweh's Graciousness') . . . He will be filled with the Holy Spirit" . . . Elizabeth conceived . . . and said, "*Yahweh* (not Zechariah) has done this for me." ' (Luke 1 :7-25)

FOLK-LORE AND THEOLOGY

There are two aspects of these stories which should be underlined in the present context. The first is the element of folk-lore. All literatures can quote examples of men who are said to have been marvellously born or providentially brought up. These are the folk heroes, who are marked out in this way as people out of the ordinary : Romulus and Remus suckled and raised by a she-wolf, Oedipus saved from apparent death by exposure, the infants Sargon and Moses miraculously preserved in reed baskets on the river. Such stories are not proved true or false by producing the basket, but by whether or not they were in actual fact great men.

But there is a second aspect to the stories. It is not unconnected with the preceding, but because it delves very much deeper it can be called theological. These men are the gift of God. This is in all truth something which can be said of every man. The believer cannot see any child as the product merely of human endeavour and natural resources. There is a graciousness about every birth which makes of it, to the eyes of faith, a creative act of God, a manifestation of the same Spirit which hovered over the primeval waters and brought life out of chaos.

But if this must be said of the birth of every man, how much more must it be said of those who were the saviours of their people? The world's redemption can never be merited or earned. It is always effected by the free act of a gracious God. Because God justifies the weak, the helpless and the sinner, not the self-sufficient, the strong and those who are in no need of salvation. And the fact that this happens again and again, that is the 'miracle', the ever renewed new creation. And whether or not this statement of faith applies in a particular way to a certain man cannot be proved by producing a photograph, only by answering the question, 'Was he or was he not a Godsend?'

It should be noted that nothing has, as yet, been said about whether these 'Godsends' are to be explained in natural or supernatural terms. In fact all the births referred to in the above texts were what we would have to call 'natural', even though the writers have chosen, for their theological purpose, to describe them as 'supernatural'. It is an indication that our distinction between natural and supernatural is too clearcut for the biblical writers, for whom the overshadowing of the Spirit of God was not an alternative to normal parenthood, because they did not think of God's activity as excluding man's, or man's God's. Later Jewish writers like Philo of Alexandria (20 B.C.) placed even more emphasis on this continuity between God's work and man's, and were able to comment on the utterly 'human' birth described in Genesis and 1 Samuel in these words : 'Isaac was begotten by the *Lord*, not as the result of (exclusively human) generation'; 'Samuel was born of a mother who was pregnant after receiving *divine* seed.'

VIRGINITY AND POVERTY

Another theme which provides the background against which the story of the virgin birth must be understood is that of poverty, which has already been shortly referred to above in the chapter on Luke's Christmas story.

It is a theme which runs the whole length of the Bible, from the writings of the first prophets down to the end of the New Testament. At first, as a merely social problem arising out of Israel's gradual settlement and urbanization in the time of the early monarchy, poverty was often seen as no more than a curse, a punishment for sin, not least of laziness. But with the increased exploitation of the depressed classes during the time of Israel's 'prosperity', the prophets found themselves more and more taking the side of the poor against their oppressors, and seeing that the beggar could be a parable of how man stands before God.

By the sixth century B.C. the word for the poor, the *anawim*, had become a technical term to describe man's religious attitude in the sight of God. The rich man in his security and self-sufficiency can deceive himself into an attitude which is to all intents and purposes one of atheism. The poor man knows that he has nothing to rely on but providence, and that he eats, as it were, out of God's hand. So the word *anawim* was increasingly used to describe the true Israel, those who knowing that they have no resources of their own to depend on are open to the saving power of God, and wait on him with abandonment, trust, humility and faith. This is the sense in which the word 'poor' is used in many of the Psalms, in Jeremiah, in the songs of the Suffering Servant, in Job, in the *Magnificat* and in the Beatitudes.

Jesus called himself poor in that sense and, although he did not simply identify his situation with economic poverty, nevertheless did live a life marked by material poverty. Many of his followers from the beginning chose a similar way of life in deliberate imitation of him, in the conviction that only one who has experienced beggarliness, helplessness, humiliation and suffering knows God as he is and stands before God as he should – in desperate need of the help which God alone can give. The theme is well summed up in a phrase from the psalter : 'Before I was afflicted I went astray.' (Psalm 119 :67) Suffering is not, as it is so often taken to be, an unmitigated disaster : it can be the road which leads to God. And when it does, then the poor are indeed blessed : The Kingdom of God is theirs.

The biblical theme of virginity is very closely connected with this theme of poverty. For many Christians with close on two thousand years' history of virginity behind them, the word conjures up something admirable, lovely and lovable. But for the Bible the word means the very opposite. There, the lovable thing is marriage. This is what is fruitful and life-giving. The virgin is the person who is fruitless, deprived and even pitiable, because she contributes nothing. Virginity is a state not of honour but of desolation and humiliation. The words 'Virgin Zion' do not mean pure, spotless, immaculate, fruitful Zion, but on the contrary 'poor Zion, pitiful Zion, wretched Zion, beggarly Zion, empty Zion'.

Perhaps the point could best be made by quoting a few lines from the Litany of Loreto, which we Catholics have long been used to say or sing in honour of our Lady :

> Virgin most prudent
> Virgin most venerable
> Virgin most renowned
> Virgin most powerful
> Virgin most faithful

Speaking *biblically* these are entirely the wrong categories, as if virginity was something to be proud of and kept intact. On the contrary, in biblical terms we would have to say :

> Virgin most foolish!
> Virgin most humiliated!
> Virgin most despised!
> Virgin most weak!
> Virgin most fruitless!

Yet it is this very condition of empty barrenness which God makes fruitful. This has been the constant theme of the Old Testament. Indeed, there is a sense in which only a virgin can give birth to God's gift. Because what God has to give cannot be achieved by human powers alone. The divine is not something which is of man's making. Only God can bring life out of an empty womb — or an empty tomb.

The climax of this theme is to be seen on Calvary, where the dead Christ is the very embodiment of poverty and powerlessness. Yet it is there that God's power is most richly shown, in the new life to which he raises his Son. Death is paired with resurrection : one is the condition of the other.

Similarly virginity is paired with motherhood : one is the prerequisite of the other. For virginity is a symbol of the salvation that is a gracious gift, the new creation which can be effected by God alone. And motherhood is the symbol of the fact that this salvation which is an unmerited new creation must be received and grow within mankind.

THE MEANING OF THE VIRGIN BIRTH

The context, therefore, in which we should be thinking when we speak of the virgin birth is that of the Old Testament 'miraculous' births, poverty, virginity made fertile, and the death and resurrection of Jesus. There

can be no doubt that those Old Testament themes are
in the mind of Luke, who actually quotes the phrase
from the Sarah story that 'nothing is impossible to God'
(Genesis 18 : 14, Luke 1 : 37), and refers the reader, as we
have seen, to the stories of Samson, Samuel, the Virgin
Zion and John the Baptist as the background against
which alone the birth of Jesus can be properly understood. Similarly, there can be no doubt that the New
Testament story of the empty tomb had influenced the
telling of the birth of Jesus; the whole gospel is a pro-
clamation of the resurrection, the opening chapters included. Finally, there can be no doubt that it was not
his virginal birth which made Jesus' disciples acclaim
him as divine. The force of the argument was exactly
the other way round : it was because they had experienced him as one risen from the dead that they were
able to recognize him and speak of him as *the* Godsend.

What then does the story of the virgin birth mean?
It means that, of all men, Jesus is the one who comes to
us from God. From what his disciples had experienced
of him in his life and teaching and death and resurrection, they concluded that of all the divine births of
which they had read here was the one which was most
truly God-given, that this was most truly God's gift to
the world, however it took place on the level of history.

It means that Jesus is God's gift through and through.
He is not merely God-like, or the noblest of men : they
had discovered him to be the complete expression of God,
a non-distorting mirror of God at work, one who brings
God utterly. They had seen that his whole life is of God,
that his being is rooted in God alone, that he is not 'of
the world' but 'of love'. In him they had seen something
of the final mystery of life itself : they had touched rock.

God shone through him, and of such a man all you
could say was that his life was fathered in Mary by the

very Spirit of God. His birth and life could not be thought of simply as biological events; his significance lay much deeper. He was the beginning of a new Israel, with a new Sarah for his mother, and a future only from God.

This is not to rationalize the story and take all the mystery out of it. As we have seen above in reference to the angels in the story, to imagine that the mystery can be stated in purely natural terms is to wreck the story which, here as there, requires something to lift it out of the ordinary run of things. For instance, to say that the word 'virgin' really only means a young woman, whether she is married or not, as some translations of the gospel do – this is to take all the meaning out of the story which, *as a story* needs a virgin, needs the intervention of God to accomplish something which man cannot achieve on his own, and needs the assurance that God really is at work here, and that this is not a 'natural' event, if the word 'natural' means something which takes place without the activity of God.

HOW DOES GOD ACT?

However the question can still be asked, 'How does God act?' Even if we grant that we are not dealing here with an event which does not require the intervention of God, we still need to know what exactly is involved in God's intervention and whether God's activity replaces or supersedes or excludes the activity of nature. If it is clear that the *story* as such requires God to be visibly and tangibly present and active, people are still entitled to ask what this presence and activity would have looked like outside the story, at the physical and biological level. Everything that has so far been said about the virgin birth is

compatible with an ordinary and non-miraculous motherhood, just as what Christians most deeply believe about
the risen Christ is compatible both with a tomb that was
found empty and with a tomb that remained occupied.
What could have been photographed or analysed under
a microscope?

Some would answer that they do not know and that
there are no means of knowing. Nor is it important,
because the biological fact is entirely secondary. No one
can absolutely exclude the possibility of someone giving
birth while remaining biologically a virgin; this is precisely what the profession of faith means that 'nothing is
impossible to God'. But this biological fact, whatever it
may have been, is beyond the reach of the historian and
the exegete, and remains secondary to the theological
fact, which is Jesus' unique relationship with God.

There are theologians who would wish to give a more
positive answer to the question and maintain that there
was no virginal birth in the literal sense outside the story.
This they would maintain on three grounds.

Firstly because of a world-view, a conviction about the
way things are. At a time when the world was seen as
partly natural and partly supernatural, an inconsistent
reality with gaps in it through which supernatural agencies entered to manipulate it, there was no difficulty in
taking 'supernatural' language absolutely literally, as if
it was a factual description of the way things actually
are. But once the world is seen as homogeneous and consistent, as autonomous and explicable in terms of itself,
without recourse to outside agencies like angels, spirits
or demons, then supernatural language can no longer be
taken literally.

Men today search for an understanding of their world
in the conviction that what at one time seemed extraordinary has today become ordinary, that 'miracles' re-

cede as 'science' advances. In such a world-view, the language of the supernatural can only be taken, most respectfully, as a symbol for the transcendence of the God who is at the heart of our world, letting it be, letting it slowly become what it is destined to be, without needing to break its continuity from time to time to assure people he is around. The virgin birth is part of such language.

Secondly (and this is simply an elaboration of the first reason) because of a growing understanding about how God acts in his world – not in the gaps left by nature but in and through nature. For instance, there was a time when it was thought that God could only be called 'creator' if he intervened directly to bring into being the creatures that make up the world, not least man himself. But there are very few who would hold that today. Most people realize that, though the concept of 'creator' needs to be expressed with more sophistication, the doctrine of creation is quite compatible with an evolutionary view of the world.

Similarly, the Old Testament birth stories quoted above have shown that the activity of God does not exclude the activity of man. To say 'God is acting' does not mean that nature is not acting. They are not in competition with each other. God's action is not something that goes on behind or between the processes of nature and history. God simply *is* the inside of these processes.

When people rightly find difficulty in accepting a God whose activity is added to the world's, when stories of God's intervention, taken literally, make God less credible to them, not more so, when they find such a concept of God irrelevant to the world they live in, even harmful, it is surely important to let them hear a language about God which does not put them in the position of having to reject God. This they have a right to expect especially from Christians, whose basic doctrine of incarnation should mean precisely that the supernatural cannot be found anywhere else except embodied in the natural. The virgin birth, taken literally, would mean that the first Christian statement about Christ must nullify that basic conviction : here the divine had to bypass the human.

The third reason why some theologians are unwilling to take the virgin birth literally is because they are concerned to safeguard the humanity of Jesus, without which the Christian has no starting point for his theology. The New Testament describes Jesus as 'made like his brethren in every respect' (Hebrews 2 : 17). This would scarcely be an adequate description of him if his life began in a way quite unlike that of his brethren. If he comes into the world not as we do, as part of the evolutionary process, but as an intruder from outside, then it is difficult to see how he could be called human except in appearance. And if his humanity is compromised, then his divinity is too, because the only entrance to that divinity, mystery as it is, is through his humanity.

DIVINITY AND ABNORMALITY

Some will fear that while such talk might very well safeguard the humanity of Jesus, it has allowed his divinity to evaporate. The explanation offered above certainly ensures that Jesus remains utterly one with us. But if he was as human and as normal as all that, then there is no reason to call him more divine than any other man. If his birth was not literally virginal, what is there to distinguish him from other men?

It must be repeated that what the New Testament

says of the divinity of Jesus is not dependent on his
'virginal birth'. In fact it is exactly the other way round.
Men were convinced that Jesus was the Son of God not
by being told that he had no human father, but by what
they saw in him. What they saw in him was a life that
was lived 'not of the flesh but of God'. And it was this
that made them describe his birth *as if* he had no human
father. But this 'as if' remains an 'as if'; they do not
hesitate to place the story of his virgin birth right next
to his genealogy, which marks him out as belonging to
the lineage of Joseph.

The uniqueness of Christ must not be looked for in
some abnormality. The New Testament speaks of him
as the uniquely normal human being, expressing in his
life the norm upon which all men are called to model
themselves. The language it uses of him was not meant
to deny that humanity, but on the contrary to underline
the significance of it, to emphasize that his life cannot be
told simply in terms of history and geography, only of
God's purpose and plan. We must not misread that language in such a way as to destroy that humanity, which
is our one life-line to the God who has been revealed in
it.

For the miracle which the New Testament calls its
readers to believe in is not some mere physical marvel,
but the utterly gracious presence and action of God in
Christ. Of that divine presence and action the story of
the virgin birth is an expression. It is not primarily a
Mariological statement, but a Christological one, a profession of faith in the love of God which has been made
manifest in Christ, reaching out to man in his poverty-
stricken need of redemption.

THE CHURCH'S TEACHING

Perhaps this chapter could best be concluded by returning to the theme with which it began. Many people
when they first come across the ideas opened up in this
chapter experience a sense of shock. That it should even
be possible to discuss the subject strikes them as a kind
of desecration. They are astonished that the constant and
uninterrupted Catholic tradition about the literal virginity of our Lady should now suddenly be questioned.
They are scandalized that a doctrine which has so frequently been defined by the Catholic Church's highest
authority[1] should be treated as an open question, as if no
decision had ever been taken on it at all.

It is my own personal view that the solemn teaching
of the Catholic Church has added nothing to what
scripture has to say on this subject. When the Church
has made its profession of faith in the virgin birth, it has
most often been content to express itself in the words
and imagery of scripture, presumably intending thereby
to state nothing other than scripture did, since no other
source of information exists. Where other documents,
official and unofficial, have gone beyond scripture in
order to discuss, mostly in the fourth and fifth centuries,
the extent of Mary's virginity during and after the birth
of Jesus, they have done so on the assumption that the

---

[1] Not so frequently, in actual fact. The title 'Virgin Mary' or
'Blessed Mary Ever-Virgin' is used with unvarying regularity
whenever Mary is referred to in creeds and councils, but the
doctrine becomes the subject of an explicit solemn definition
only at Constantinople II (A.D.553) and Lateran IV (A.D.1215).
The local councils held at the Lateran in 649 and at Toledo in
675 use the same language, as also does Pope Paul IV in his
condemnation of Unitarianism in 1555.

scriptural imagery was to be taken literally and was therefore subject to this sort of scrutiny.

Yet even these strange speculations had at their heart a deeper concern : to safeguard the precious truth about Jesus which scripture had expressed in terms of the virgin birth. It is this fundamental message, rather than the language in which it has been conveyed in Church documents through the ages, which should occupy our attention, namely that Jesus is *par excellence* the gift of God to men and the act of God among men, that he is the Son of God in a way no other son of man has been, and that therefore his significance is deeper than could be conveyed by describing his birth, life and death in merely natural terms. And this is something which we would wish to affirm, and no less strongly, even if the Christmas stories had never been written, and even if the image of a virgin birth had never been thought of.

I would conclude therefore by returning to the hypothetical questioner whom I earlier imagined asking me, 'Do you believe in the virgin birth?' In the light of all that has been said in this chapter, I can only answer, 'Of course I do! I believe in what that story means, because it expresses for me all that Christ means to me. The words "the Blessed Virgin Mary" will always speak to me of the emptiness and poverty of mankind filled to overflowing by a God who is sheer grace. Nor would this faith of mine be shaken if (*per impossibile*) someone were to produce conclusive evidence that Jesus was born in the ordinary course of nature, because this faith does not depend on, less still consist of, a biological fact.'

And if what has been said in this chapter is a cause of surprise to some of my fellow-Christians, they can at least take comfort from the fact that when they hear it said again by others (as they will), they will no longer be startled as if by something new.

8. Postscript

In the week of 23 October 1972, I was asked by the B.B.C. to take part in a series of short radio talks entitled 'Christianity, Dead or Alive?' The series had already dealt with the death and resurrection of Jesus as the centre of the Christian message. My own talks were to deal with the Christmas stories as a commentary of the evangelists on a Jesus who had died but remained ever alive for them. Since these talks express in the simplest terms I could manage the gist of what I have tried to say in this book, I append them here as a postscript.

THE CHRISTMAS STORIES AND THE RESURRECTION

I have just come back from America, and there they told me the story of a Religious Information Centre in North Carolina which had on display in its window a large picture of the dead Christ in the arms of his mother. An old Negro lady opened the door and pushed her head round the corner.

'That Jesus dead in your window?'

'Yes.'

'He done been killed by the bad mans?'

'Yes.'

'Done dead and gone for ever, that poor Jesus done gone and dead for ever, huh?'

'No, he rose again on Easter morning.'

'Rose again? You mean he live again? He rise from the dead? He really truly rise from the dead?'

'Yes – you must have heard the story of the resurrection before.'

And with a broad smile, her face bubbling with joy, the old lady said, 'Oh, I done heard it before. I guess I done heard it a million times before. But I just glories to hear it again.'

If you were listening to 'Thought for the Day' any time during the last two weeks, I sincerely hope you will have been glorying to hear it again and again, this death and resurrection of Jesus which, Christians believe, tells them all that they really want to know or to say about him.

And that's true even of those Christians who wrote the opening chapters of the gospels, which tell the story of Jesus' birth and infancy. It is because of what happened to Jesus in his death and resurrection that these writers felt the need to describe his birth as something stupendous, something momentous.

If we don't take the death and resurrection of Jesus as our starting point, as the gospel writers did, these pages of theirs will read like fairy tales – these stories of angels, and miraculous births, and skies opening, and messages from heaven. But the Bible is not about remarkable things happening in the sky. It's about us, and the love God has for us, and the way that love was proved in the life of Jesus. God was in Jesus. And Jesus lives on with us, beyond his death, to put that deep mystery which we call God always within our grasp. Men who believe that about Jesus won't want to soft-pedal what they say about his birth.

You'll remember the story of the wicked king Herod trying to get rid of the child by slaughtering all the babes in Bethlehem. That's really an echo of the Moses story, when he escaped the plans of the wicked Pharaoh to murder all the Hebrew children. It's a story which says: Jesus is a new Moses, born to lead people out of slavery.

You'll remember the title given to the infant Jesus as he's born in Bethlehem, 'King of the Jews'. That's really an echo of the David story – David the Bethlehem shepherd who became the greatest king the Jews ever had. It's a story which says: Jesus is a new David, bringing that peace which all men long for.

And you'll remember the story of the wise men, following a star from the east and finding the child and offering him their gifts. That's really an echo of the Solomon story, where kings and queens came from the east to offer him their gifts, and where the queen of Sheba (so Jewish writings said) was led to him by a star. It's a story which says: Behold a greater than Solomon here.

A new Moses, a new David, a new Solomon. All that was most worthwhile about their past history. That's what his disciples had discovered Jesus to be in his life, in his preaching, and in their experience of his continued presence with them after his death. No wonder they wrote of his birth with such enthusiasm.

Jesus is alive, still, today. Jesus is God's gift to the world, the Godsend for which Christians can never stop being thankful. These stories of his infancy, like the rest of the gospel, continue to speak that message to us across the centuries.

WHAT REALLY HAPPENED?

I was saying yesterday that if we don't allow for the fact

that the gospels were written after Jesus' resurrection, and in the light of all that his disciples experienced the risen Jesus to be, then the stories they tell of his birth and infancy will sound like fairy tales. It's because I know that a lot of people do regard them as fairy tales, and dismiss them as unworthy of their consideration, that I'm anxious to say more on this subject. I want to try to show something of the depth contained in these apparently naïve stories.

You see, supposing you and I had been present at Jesus' birth, and someone asked us, 'What really happened?', we might have replied, 'Well, nothing out of the ordinary. A Jewish builder, his wife, poor people, a baby was born.'

Now the gospel writer would say to that, 'What a shallow way of looking at it! Why don't you look deeper? In the light of all that this child eventually proved to be, in view of all that came out of this event, are you just going to say "a baby was born"? How about a bit of excitement? What really happened? What *really* happened was that the Son of God was born, and the whole of the heavens rejoiced. This was *the* decisive moment in history. God was in this apparently trivial event. I can't use humdrum language to say that.'

But now do you see what happens? If you and I are naïve in the way we read his account, and don't appreciate the poetry as poetry, we've returned to the shallow level we started with. We'll say, 'Your account is all about angels and stars and voices. It's all about the kind of things which never happen in the sort of world I live in. What really happened? Obviously something which is nothing like the sort of things that happen to me.'

But the truth is that what happened is exactly like what happens to you and me, in exactly the sort of world we live in, if only you and I had the eyes to see it.

This is terribly important to understand, otherwise we gradually lose touch with God altogether. God no one has ever seen. But if he really is in contact with us, if he really does enter into a relationship with us, we've got to speak in concrete images and express ourselves in visual terms. And that's what the Bible does. What else can a poet do? But if we take those images literally, as if God's activity really was visible, then the Bible becomes a never-never-land.

You imagine how Alf Garnett's son-in-law might put it – if he toned his language down a bit. 'Believe in the Bible? All right for kids. They taught me the Bible at school, and they expected me to believe that once upon a time God walked the earth, and talked with men, as if you could have filmed it! They told me that Moses saw God in the burning bush, and spoke with him on the mountain, as if anyone else, if he'd been there, could have joined in the conversation! And then that long conversation that Mary had with the Angel of the Lord; you'd think someone was there with his microphone getting it all down on tape! And all that stuff about the Holy Spirit coming down on Jesus at his baptism, and all the strange, weird happenings which proved that God was interfering in his life all the time!'

And Alf's son-in-law might add, 'If you believe that, you'll believe anything! I know the sort of world we live in. So do you. It's a world where innocent babies die, and even your Jesus got crucified, and God didn't do a thing. It's a world where six million Jews were burned in ovens, and there weren't any miracles to save them!'

Surely there's something in this objection. We live in a world where God is hidden, and we can't see him. We can only know of his presence in faith. It's a world where nothing interrupts the order of nature. Our lives are very ordinary lives. What use could we have for a religion which was out of this world? We need something which tells us what our ordinary lives are about. We can't be helped by hearing about people who saw what we can't see.

I really believe that the Bible isn't trying to tell us about another fancy world. I believe that it really does, in its picturesque way, tell us about ordinary people like you and me, living through the ordinary events that you and I know, only they saw them in depth, with the eyes of faith.

The Bible tells us above all about Jesus, and it tells us that he is like you and me. It's by looking at Jesus that I really see what I can be. Jesus is the truth about us. If he were not, if he were only some visitor from outer space, how could what is written about him be good news for us?

ANGELS IN THE CHRISTMAS STORIES

Have you ever wondered why it is that the stories of Jesus' childhood contain so many angels? There's the angel who informs Zechariah about the birth of his son John, and the angel who foretells the birth of Mary's son Jesus, and the angel who advises Joseph to accept Mary's pregnancy. Then there are the angels who announce the good news to the shepherds in the fields, and the angel who warns Joseph of the danger he's in from Herod, and the angel who comes back to give him the all-clear.

The only other page of the gospel which has anything like this number of angels is the story of the resurrection, where they're mentioned seven times. In the rest of the gospel story the angels are very scarce. In fact, they've got no walking-on part at all, except once in the story of Jesus' temptation in the desert, and once in the account of his agony in the garden.

Now there are two events which, the story says, had no witnesses. Isn't it worth asking why only they are told in angel-language? And there are the two great stories (Jesus' birth and resurrection) which couldn't be recorded in the ordinary sense of the word. Isn't it worth asking why only they are described in terms of angels?

I suppose there are a number of ways of dealing with angels. One is to take them quite literally. They are an order of beings immeasurably higher than man, created by God to live in an invisible world outside our own, and coming from time to time into our world to carry out God's will. But of course, in that case, all that the angels have done is to remove God even further away from us than he would otherwise have been. And perhaps that's what those who hold this point of view want. But I'm not sure it squares very well with what the New Testament says, that in Jesus God has bound himself to be close to us for ever, and that apart from Jesus there's no more need for any mediator between God and mankind.

Another way of explaining these stories about angels would be to take all the mystery out of them and say they are really Unidentified Flying Objects. I have heard people quite seriously proposing that the human race once existed on another planet, and that we were expelled from there by being put on a space-craft which crashlanded us all on this earth. That's what Original Sin and the Fall was really about. And from then on, messages and space-craft continue to come to us from that earlier planet of ours, to give us divine guidance.

And all kinds of things in the Bible, like the Pillar of
Cloud and Elijah's fiery chariot, these, they say, were
really UFO's of this kind. And that's how we get the
star leading the magi to Bethlehem, and the vision of the
shepherds in the fields. All flying saucers.

Well! When I hear things like this, words fail me.
Science fiction has taken over from mystery. Where has
all the wonder of the story gone? What I need to break
into my life is not more nuts and bolts, more iron-
mongery than I've already experienced. I need God
himself.

And that's surely what the story of the angels at the
birth of Jesus tells me, that in the quite ordinary life
of a girl in Nazareth, and in the child she bore, where
nobody could have taped or filmed anything remarkable, the activity of God was there for anyone who
knew and believed in the end of the story as we do.

And so another way of approaching the angels is to
see them simply as a poetic language. This is a language
which tells me of God's power. To speak of angels break-
ing in is to assure me that God's power is exercised here
on earth (not in some distant heaven), and that it's a
power to protect, and support, and lead me to union
with him.

Is this to get rid of the supernatural? Would this
make our world too ordinary, incapable of being visited
by real beings from outside? Would this lock the world
inside what is human?

Let me tell you how I would prefer to put it. I think
the Christian is the one who believes that, because of
Jesus, what we call the supernatural is already locked
in the world. There is no need for outsiders. Christianity
is the bold faith which dares to say that, since Christ,
God can only be discovered on our ordinary earth, in
the life of a man who was so ordinary that most people

didn't even notice him.

And if that original insight were to be threatened by what we say about angels, we'd have to stop talking about them. But why not keep the insight, and keep the poetry of the angels?

KEEPING THE STORIES

Ten years ago, during the Roman Catholic Vatican Council, Cardinal Suenens of Belgium asked an Indian bishop,

'What do they think about the Council in India?'

'In India, they are not thinking about it at all.'

'Why?'

'Because they are not understanding anything of what the Council is talking about.'

'Well, what would they understand?'

And with a wistful look the Indian bishop said, 'Oh, if only the Council would tell us a parable.'

A parable, a story, this has always spoken to people of all cultures far more deeply than anything said in abstract language. I've been using a good deal of abstract language this week in speaking about the stories of Jesus' childhood. I now want to add that I think it's terribly important to keep the stories, and not merely the abstract language about them.

Put it this way. Those of us who are Christians are so used to thinking of Jesus as the Son of God that we sometimes find it difficult to tell others (or even ourselves) that he was, like you and me, a son of man. We say, 'He *was* a real man', not realizing that we don't say that about other men we know. If I say, 'That fellow's got real eyebrows', people will begin to think there must be some doubt about it. When we say, 'Jesus was a real man', it sounds as if what Jesus really was was God, and the human about him was only a disguise.

For the writers of the New Testament the difficulty was the other way round. They knew that what he really was *was* a man. Their problem was to find a way to express the uniqueness of this man, to find words to convey the depths that they saw in his death and resurrection. In his selfless death, they knew that in him the love of God had come among men, completely. In their experience of the same Jesus living on beyond death, they knew that God was in Christ, reconciling the world to himself.

They wrote of him in that light, in the light of all they had experienced him to be. Their writings speak to our faith, we who have shared that experience with them.

I say this because I'm worried that, over this week, I might have given the impression that if Jesus really is one of us, then it's no longer worthwhile reading these stories of his infancy which seem to make him someone quite unlike us. If there was no magic about his conception and birth, if there was no photographable star or opening of the heavens, if there were no tape-recordable angels singing the glory of God, if there was nothing patently supernatural about these events at all, why waste time reading about them?

I'll tell you. Because these stories have a power which no lecture or broadcast could ever have. When I read the story of Jesus' birth of a virgin mother, it speaks to me of the utter kindness and generosity of God, and of his creative power which can draw new life out of empty wombs and empty tombs.

When I read the story of the turmoil this child brought into people's lives – Mary, Joseph, the magi, Herod, the whole of Jerusalem and all the babes of Bethlehem – I'm forced to ask myself whether the risen Christ challenges my life in the same way.

When I read the story of the shepherds and their vision of angel choirs, I discover afresh that, in Christ, God breaks into my life.

When I read the story of the message from heaven, of glory in the highest and peace on earth, I hear an echo of the risen Christ who said just that to his disciples, 'Shalom, my peace I give to you.' And he's continued to say that to millions of his followers since.

In fact, when I read any of the gospel stories, I breathe a sigh of relief that what is most deeply true about Jesus has been preserved for me in stories which can be repeated from generation to generation, and not in abstract arguments which may be relevant today but tomorrow will be as dead as October leaves. It's through these stories that Christ continues to come to me today, and invites me to become part of the story of his life.

Just listen to this : 'The star which they had seen in the East went before them, till it came to rest over the place where the child was. When they saw the star, they rejoiced exceedingly with great joy; and going into the house they saw the child with Mary his mother, and they fell down and worshipped him.' (Matthew 2 :9-11) Am I willing to be numbered among the wise men who fall down and worship Jesus as saviour? But my question doesn't put the challenge half as strongly, or half as beautifully as the story does.